Front Cover Art Composite:

"LOVE MONSTER WITH EGG ON ITS FACE"
2000 #146
"LOVE MONSTER WITH A HAIR LIP"
1998 #89

LOVE MONSTERS
AREN'T SCARY
THEY'RE JUST MISUNDERSTOOD

THE ART OF

TONY BARONE

WRITTEN BY

KAREN & TONY BARONE

BARONE

A <u>HEART</u>FELT THANKS TO:

Letha Davis

Homeira & Arnold Goldstein

Patricia Correia Gallery

ISBN NUMBER   0-9741763-0-3

Printed in Singapore

C O N T E N T S and CAST OF CHARACTERS

PROLOGUE

Language — the beasts strive for it, but humans have it, and that's what makes us different, perhaps even interesting. But language is a tricky business and often deceives the ear. On the other hand, eyes see what they see. Imagine a parallel universe inhabited by monsters — what we don't understand, after all, becomes monstrous soon enough. Imagine further that other world is subterranean, buried in a warren of caves carved into the Hollywood Hills, under the feet of those who earn their bread with ears and eyes, words and vision. And what if humans found those caves, the home of an ancient race of monsters with heart shaped heads, those monsters who heard things differently and dazzled the eye with a vision no less real however bizarre? What then?

CHAPTER I

AN EXTRAORDINARILY PHENOMENAL DISCOVERY

"Good evening," begins Professor Dr. Conundrum, as he addresses the audience assembled in the auditorium of the County Museum of Art, "I Chair the Anthropological Studies at the State University. Thank you for inviting me here tonight and giving me an opportunity to speak to you at this time of exciting discoveries in cave art."

"A monumental and historically important find was made by the great American adventurer Reraldo Jivera. The massive cache of sexually charged wall paintings were produced by a subterranean, uncultured culture, that inhabited caves below the famed hillside houses of Hollywood, California."

"Presumably, Hollywood was selected, not only because it afforded well camouflaged hillside entrances for the cave dwellers, but because this subterranean society deduced it would not have to dig deeply because the people in Hollywood are reputed to be so shallow."

"Anthropologists and archeologists at the site have dubbed the two dimensional heavily pigmented figures represented in the cave drawings: 'LOVE MONSTERS,' or, in scientific jargon, 'Ovelay Onstersmay' (oov-lay on-sters-may), thus named because of the heart shape of their heads. It's thought that the heart shaped heads were a result of the Love Monsters thinking of themselves as sensitive creatures who thought with their hearts, or maybe, like us, they just wanted to be loved."

"Some hypothesize that the Love Monsters initially arrived on the West Coast in the trunks of Volkswagen Beetles during the 'summer of love' in the early 70's. First the Love Monsters landed in San Francisco with the hopes of getting in on the 'free love' phenomena. They were disappointed to find that they were only able to get love free with an Estee Lauder purchase. Totally frustrated they migrated to Los Angeles where nothing has value but everything has a price."

"LOVE MONSTER IN L.A. WHERE NOTHING HAS VALUE AND EVERYTHING HAS A PRICE"

"The members of this society speak to us through their art. The art on the walls of the caves displays a detailed picture of a complex homogeneous unit with fascinating social relationships."

"The contemporary cave paintings at this site reveal a previously unknown community that inhabited these subterranean dwellings. The cave paintings also illuminate one particular family unit at the center of the discovery: the Kahns."

"The majority of figurative cave art found was created by the members of the Kahn family, and was found in the Kahn-cave. We think primarily the Love Monsters' knowledge has come from watching television, where the lines between fact and fiction are blurred. For many Americans, the television was the Love Monsters' mental incubator. The Love Monsters have artfully created an alter-ego of their own society based primarily on their observations of us. This alter-ego is a visual hybrid: part them, part us. In an attempt to emulate us and fit in, they have recorded how we act and what we do, however, they don't quite get it right; they seem to literally take things literally. They only hear what you are not saying . . .something is lost in translation."

"Paleoanthropologists hypothesize that wandering bands of Love Monsters, who were escaping cold climates, evolved into a split off species of Homo erectus; however, the modern history of the Love Monsters is the subject of much debate."

"THE LOVE MONSTER'S ANCESTOR, HOMO ERECTUS"
2002 #181

"The Love Monsters' cave wall drawings appear to be genderless. Though some male and female figurative representation occurs in the cave art, the Love Monsters, with their heart shaped heads, are androgynous, so don't fuck with them."

"LOVE MONSTERS ARE ANDROGYNOUS...DON'T FUCK WITH THEM"
1998 #99

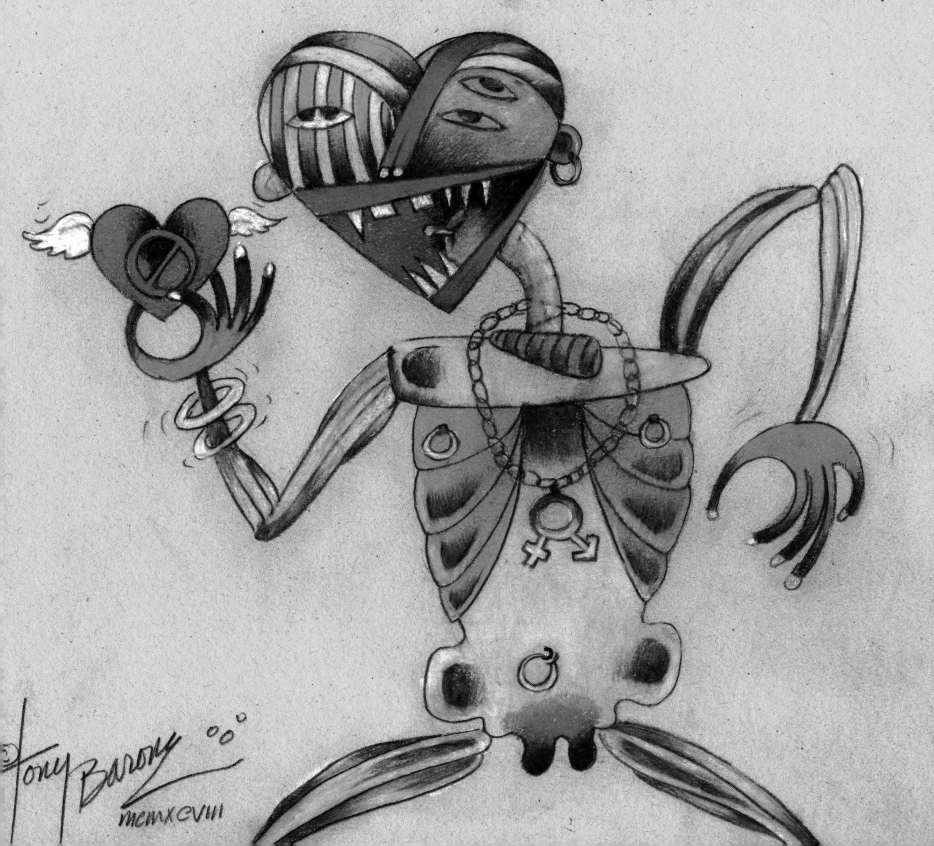

"The Love Monsters do not have familiar human genitalia. They have two cute and playful looking, often red, udder-like soft appendages dangling between their legs. We don't know what these appendages are, or how they function, but we have the urge to play with them. It looks as if the Love Monsters are born genderless, and that they later assume gender defined roles in their family units and in their community."

"Love Monsters, under pressure to appear 'normal' by California standards, used this gender assigning method to create sons and daughters. The assumption of a convenient gender title was common throughout the subterranean Love Monsters' community and allowed them to more accurately emulate us."

"The Love Monsters give birth through a reproductive process called a birth-quake. The term birth-quake was derived from overhearing a couple asking after sex: 'Did the earth move for you?'"

"BIRTH-QUAKE"
1997 #46

"BIRTH QUAKE"

CHAPTER II
XAVIER KAHN
THE KAHN FAMILY PATRIARCH

"The Love Monster that assumed the role of the patriarch of the Kahn family was Xavier Kahn, known simply as X. Kahn (many believed the X stood for Extortion). He ruled supreme over the Kahn family unit which consisted of four individuals: himself, his wife, a college-age daughter, and a pubescent son."

"Like many European family names, 'Goldsmith and Carpenter,' for example, X. Kahn got his last name from his trade: he was a con-artist. His specialty was painting portraits of ex-convicts and criminals. One of his first subjects in prison was a flaky cereal killer.

"LOVE MONSTER AS A CEREAL KILLER"
2001 #157

"In addition to selling his own art, X. Kahn would supplement his income by peddling forgeries painted by other artists. One such artist impostor was the always over-imbibing false French impressionist Too Loose Lautrec."

"TOO LOOSE LAUTREC"
1997 #53

18

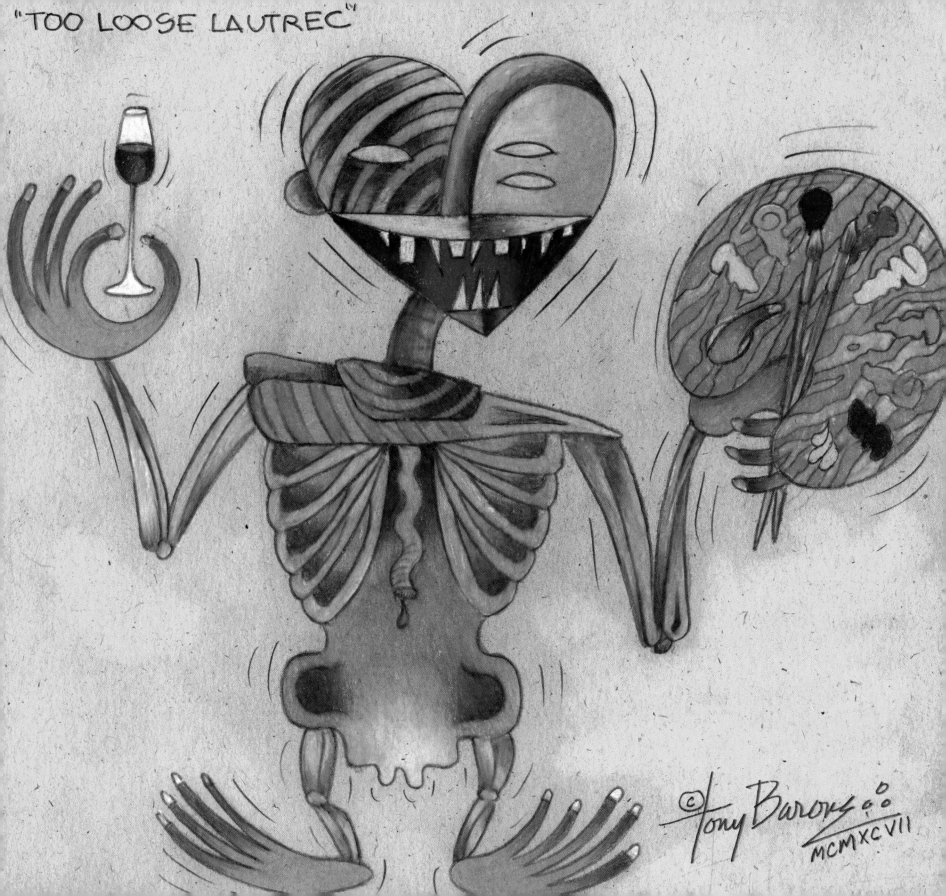

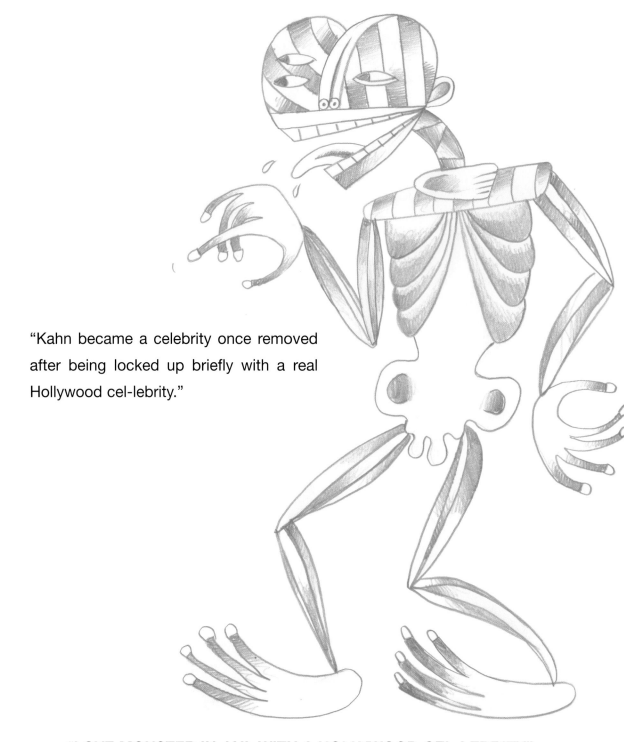

"Kahn became a celebrity once removed after being locked up briefly with a real Hollywood cel-lebrity."

"LOVE MONSTER IN JAIL WITH A HOLLYWOOD CEL-LEBRITY"
2002 #175

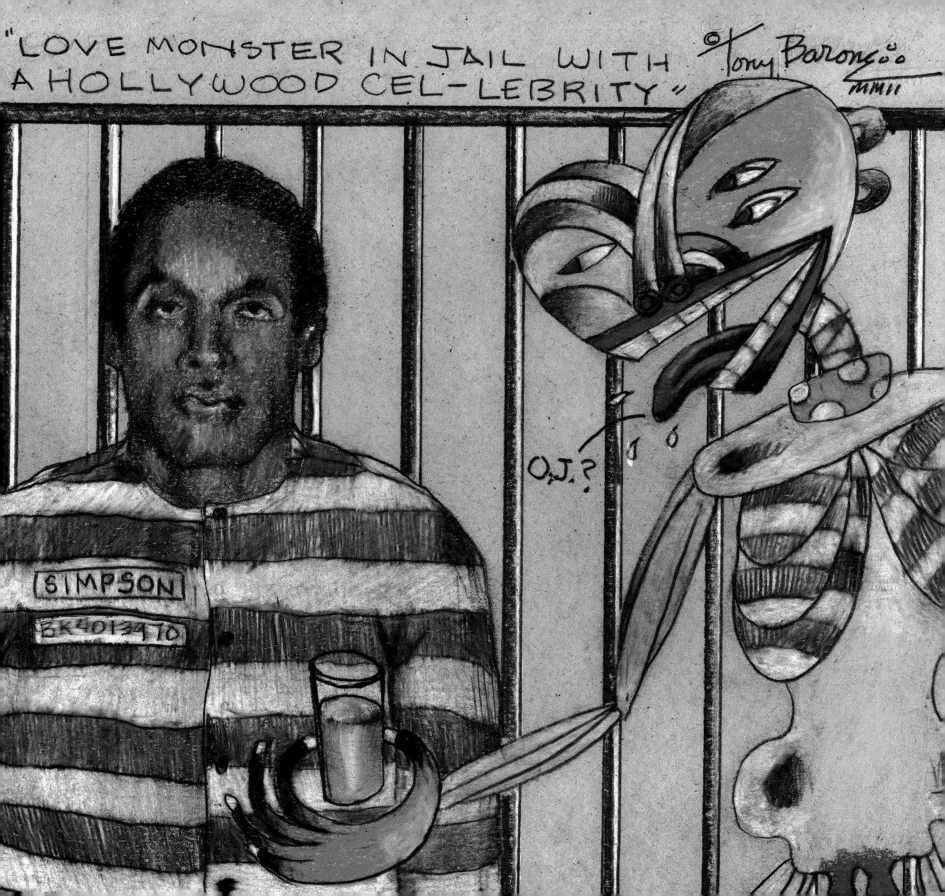

"One of Kahn's cell mates, a photographer by the name of Arsenal Adams, was incarcerated on a firearms charge for discharging his revolver at a nude photo shoot."

"LOVE MONSTER @ A NUDE PHOTO SHOOT"
1999 #132

"LOVE MONSTER @ A NUDE PHOTO SHOOT"

© Tony Baron
MCMXCIX

"X. Kahn and his second story buddies used to meet at The Crow Bar, an underworld hangout and watering hole where screwdrivers and bloody marys are popular."

"THE LOVE MONSTER HAVING A BLOODY MARY @ A CROW BAR"
2001 #161

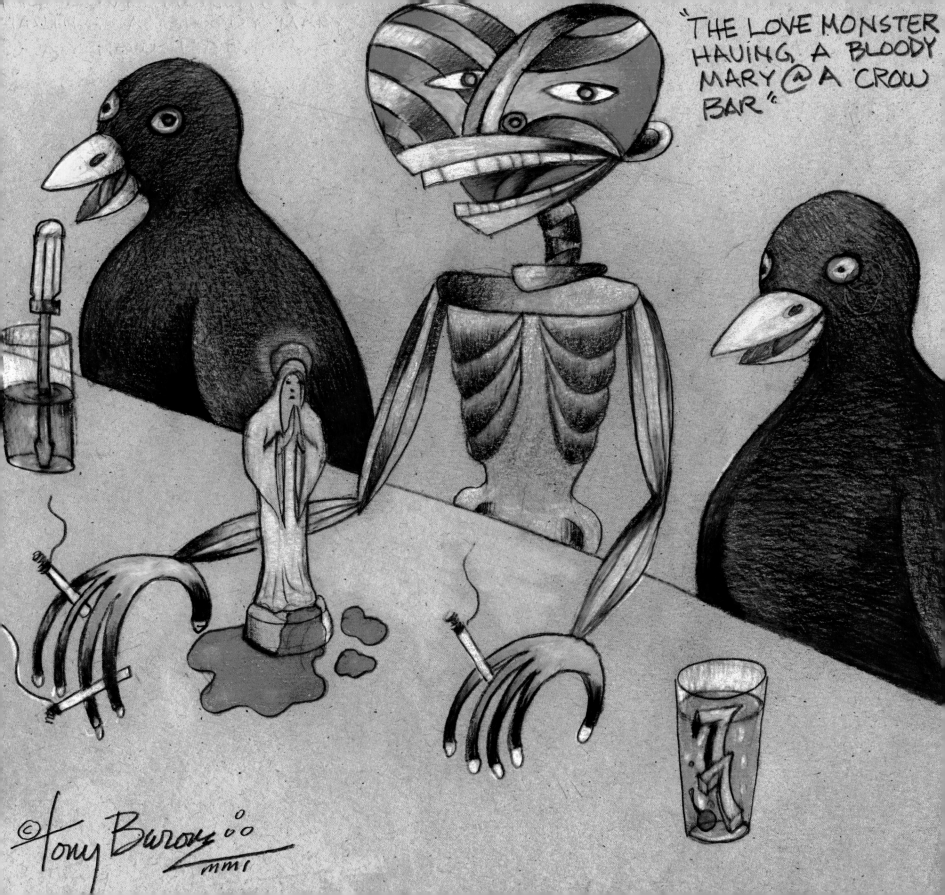

"X. Kahn loved jazz. Before he was incarcerated, when he wasn't hanging out at The Crow Bar, nothing made him happier than going to Le Club Foot, 'sitting in' and 'jamming with friends.'"

"LOVE MONSTER JAMMING w/ FRIENDS"
2002 #172

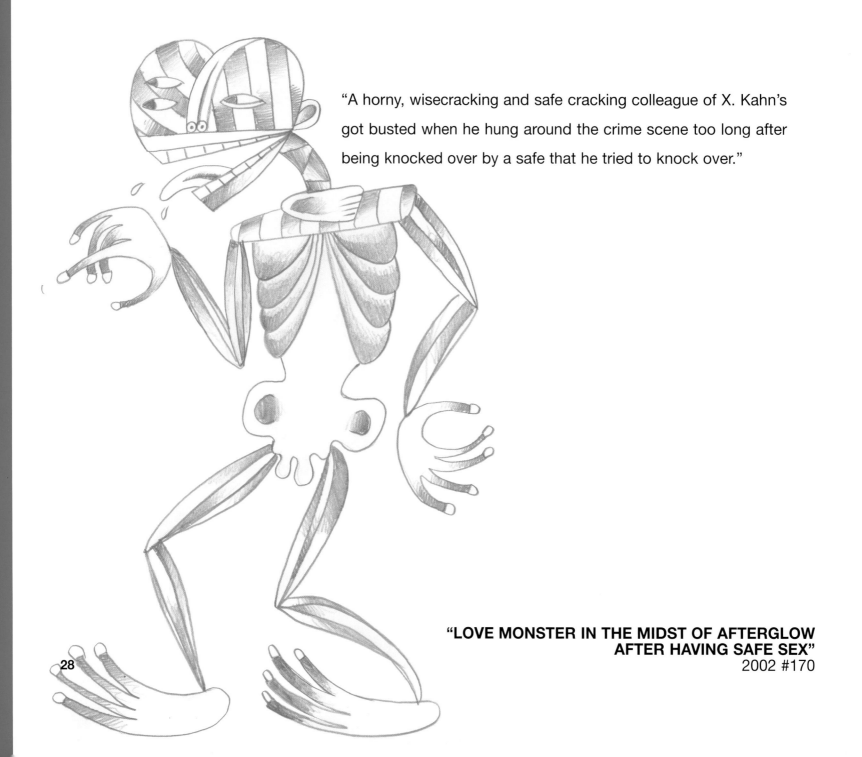

"A horny, wisecracking and safe cracking colleague of X. Kahn's got busted when he hung around the crime scene too long after being knocked over by a safe that he tried to knock over."

"LOVE MONSTER IN THE MIDST OF AFTERGLOW AFTER HAVING SAFE SEX"
2002 #170

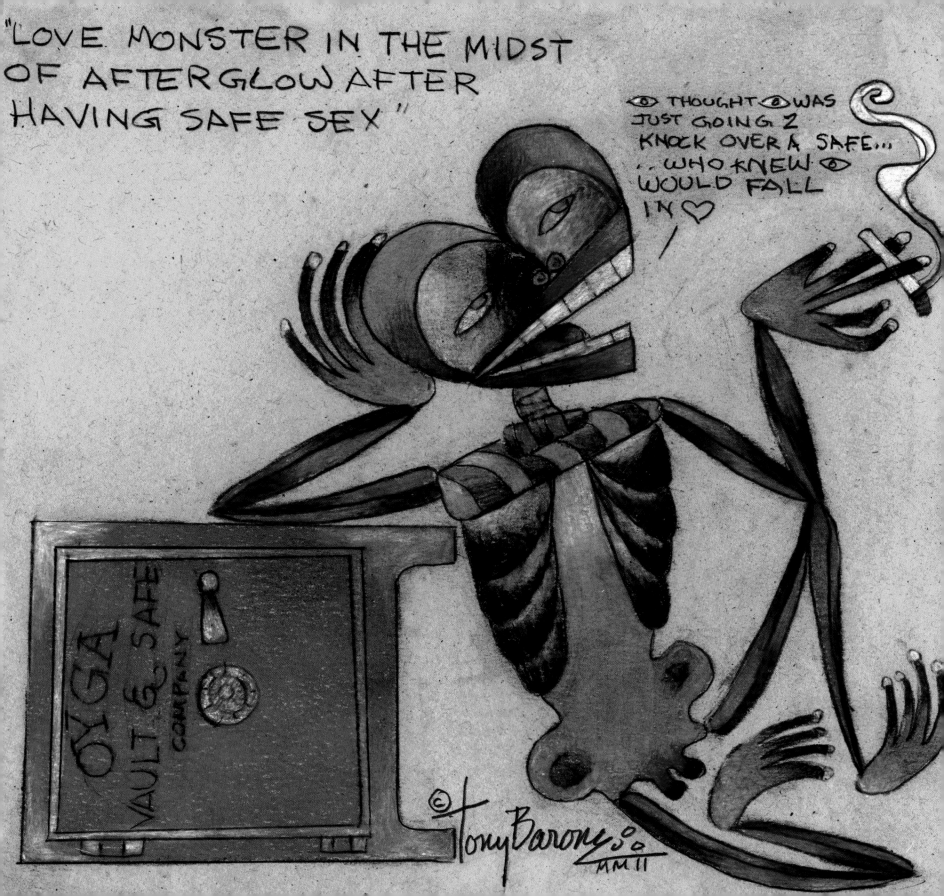

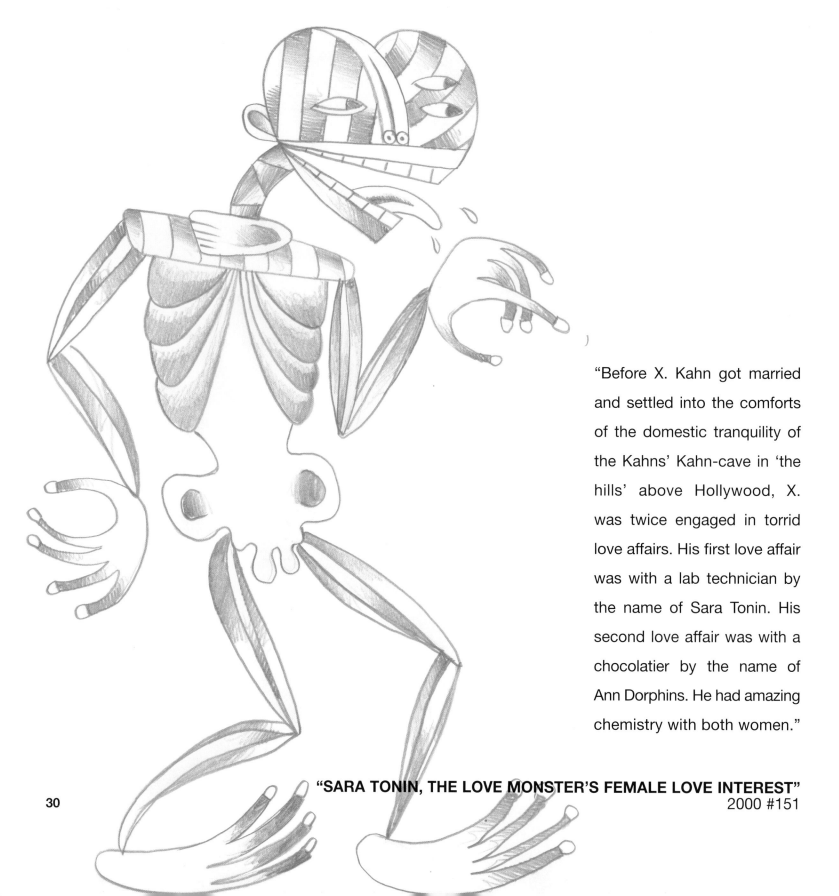

"Before X. Kahn got married and settled into the comforts of the domestic tranquility of the Kahns' Kahn-cave in 'the hills' above Hollywood, X. was twice engaged in torrid love affairs. His first love affair was with a lab technician by the name of Sara Tonin. His second love affair was with a chocolatier by the name of Ann Dorphins. He had amazing chemistry with both women."

"SARA TONIN, THE LOVE MONSTER'S FEMALE LOVE INTEREST"
2000 #151

"SARA TONIN THE LOVE MONSTER'S FEMALE LOVE INTEREST"

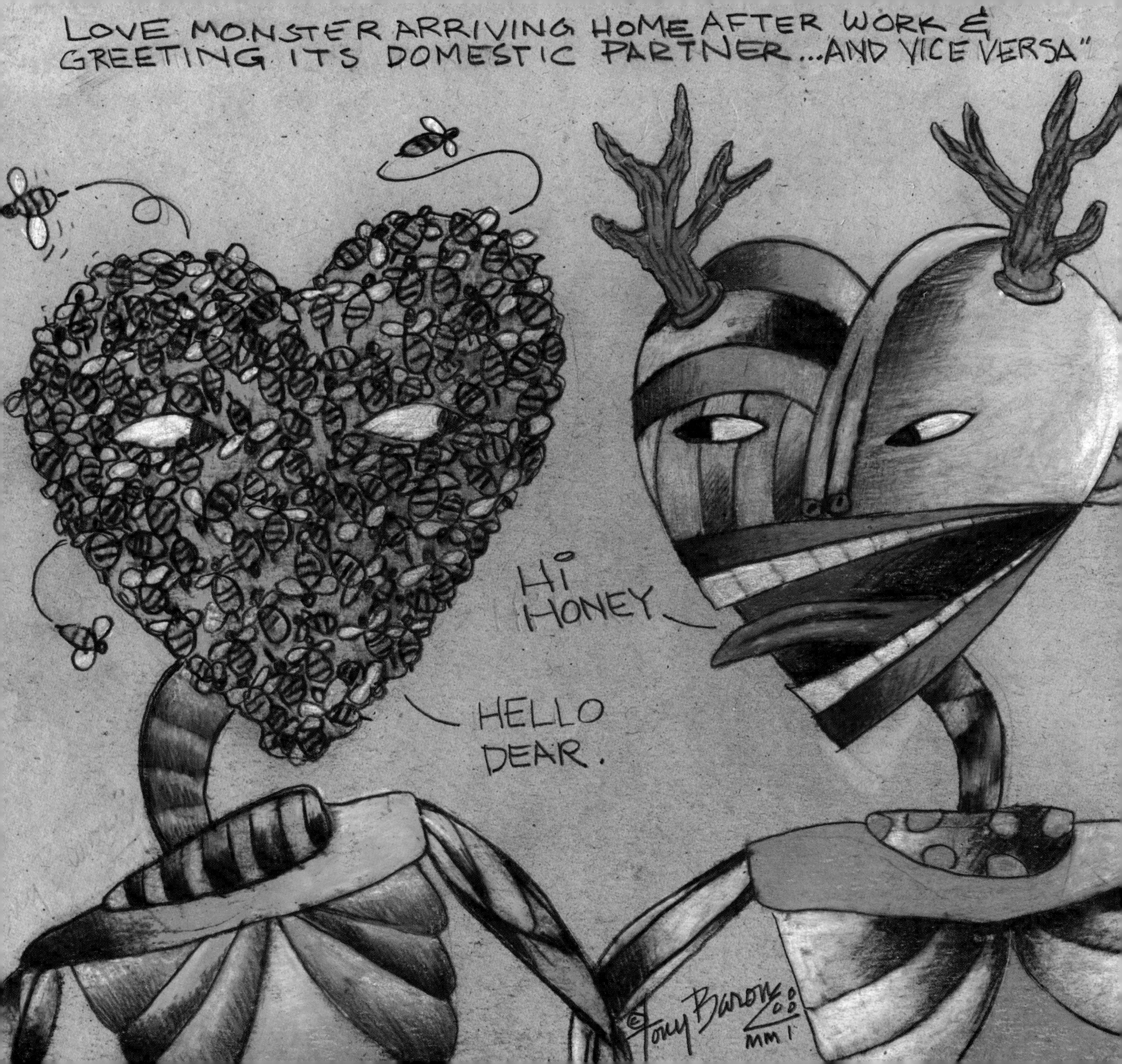

LOVE MONSTER ARRIVING HOME AFTER WORK &
GREETING ITS DOMESTIC PARTNER...AND VICE VERSA"
HI HONEY
HELLO DEAR.
©Tony Baron
MMI

CHAPTER III
EATIE WRIGHT (KAHN)

THE KAHN FAMILY UNIT MATRIARCH

"The one night stands and the great sex with Sara Tonin and Ann Dorphins were all over the day X. Kahn met 'Miss Right,' Miss Eatie Wright, who would become the love of his life."

"Eatie Wright (Kahn), the matriarch of the Kahn family unit, like many modern or professional women, chose not to take her husband's family name."

"Eatie Wright and X. Kahn were very 'lovey dovey.' They were always calling each other by pet names. When X., Eatie's ex-con husband, arrived home after work, Eatie would call him 'dear' and X. would call her 'honey.'"

"LOVE MONSTER ARRIVING HOME AFTER WORK & GREETING ITS DOMESTIC PARTNER . . . AND VICE VERSA"
2001 #155

33

"Eatie Wright, a vegetarian activist, was named by Chinese missionaries after she applied for a missionary position. At 18 years old, with a lot more than 'meats' the eye, she made the mistake of entering the Miss-Steak beauty pageant."

(MISS-STEAK)
1997 #28

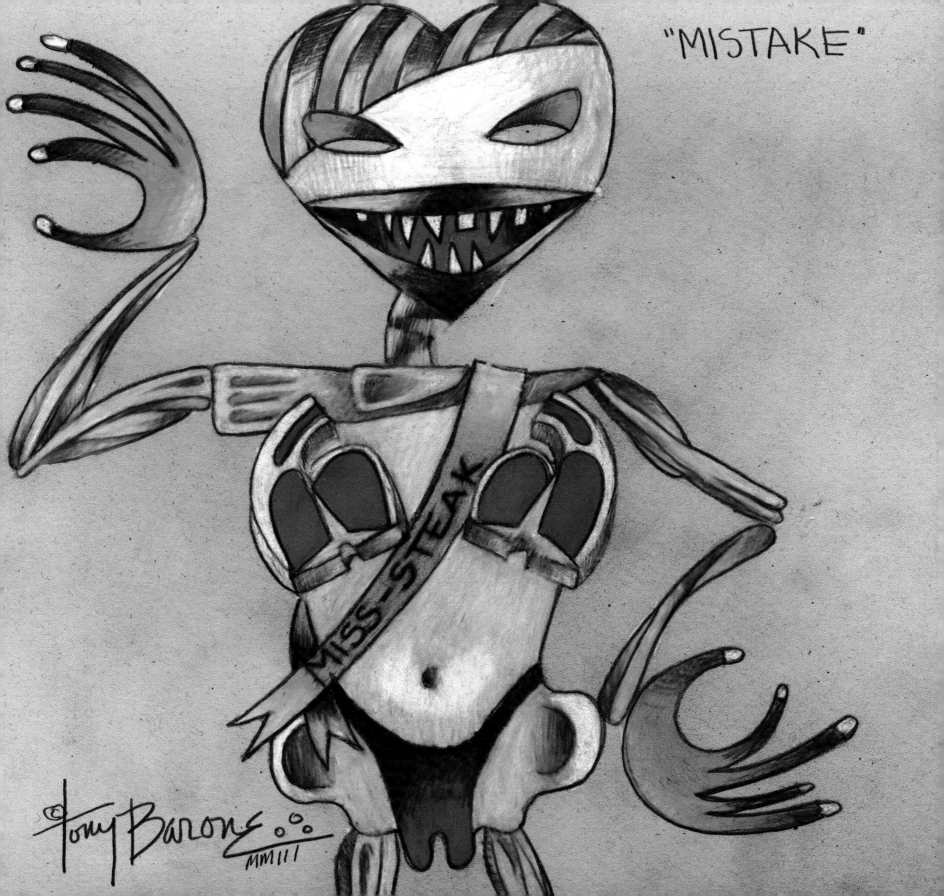

"While working at the Steak & Ail, Eatie Wright tried to direct people away from the predominately meat-laden menu and encourage them to visit the salad bar and have a non-artery-clogging lite meal."

"LOVE MONSTER ENJOYING A LITE MEAL"
2003 #206

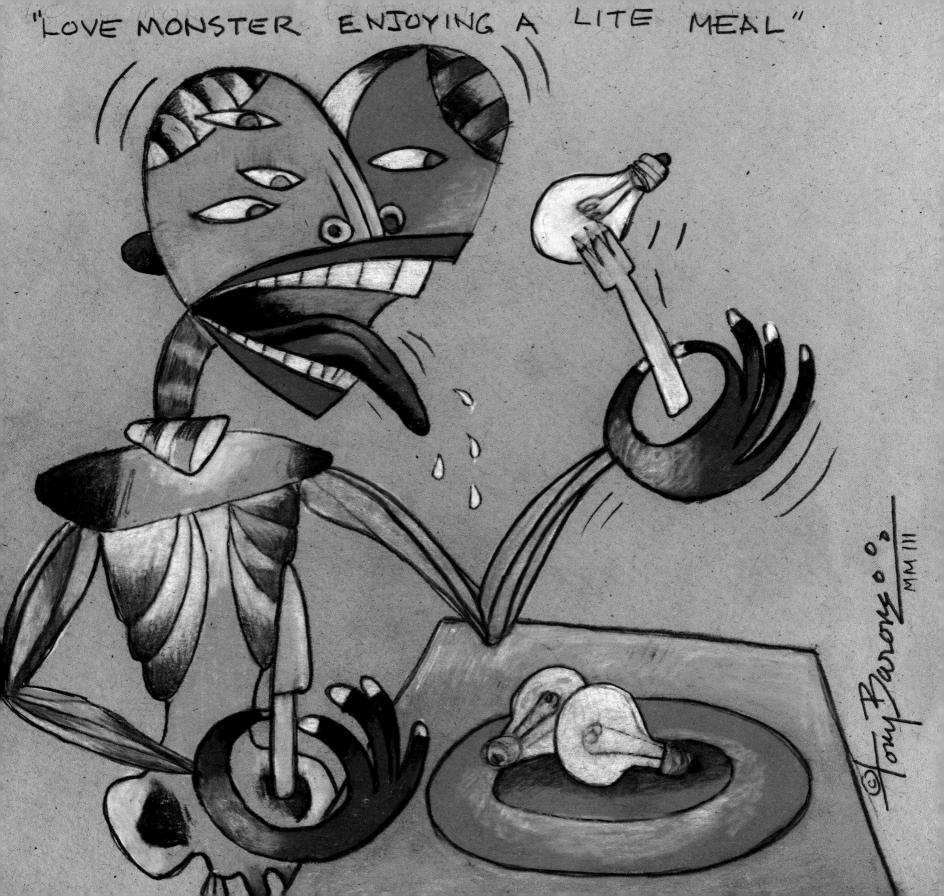

"Although Eatie works in a restaurant, she brings a toe-fu lunch from home. Brown bagging it forces her to forego her employee food allowance and foot the bill."

"LOVE MONSTER EATING TOE-FU"
1998 #86

"LOVE MONSTER
EATING TOE-FU"

©Tony Barody
MCMXCVII

"In a war of words, where a love monster was in a confrontation with a chicken, Eatie Wright sided with the chicken."

"LOVE MONSTER IN A CONFRONTATION WITH A CHICKEN"
1999 #108

"Interested in both Eastern and Western spiritual thought, Eatie Wright romantically practiced ancient and new wave religions. She frequently prayed and requested divine intervention from her heavenly patron Saint Mary Wanna."

"SAINT MARY WANNA"
1997 #47

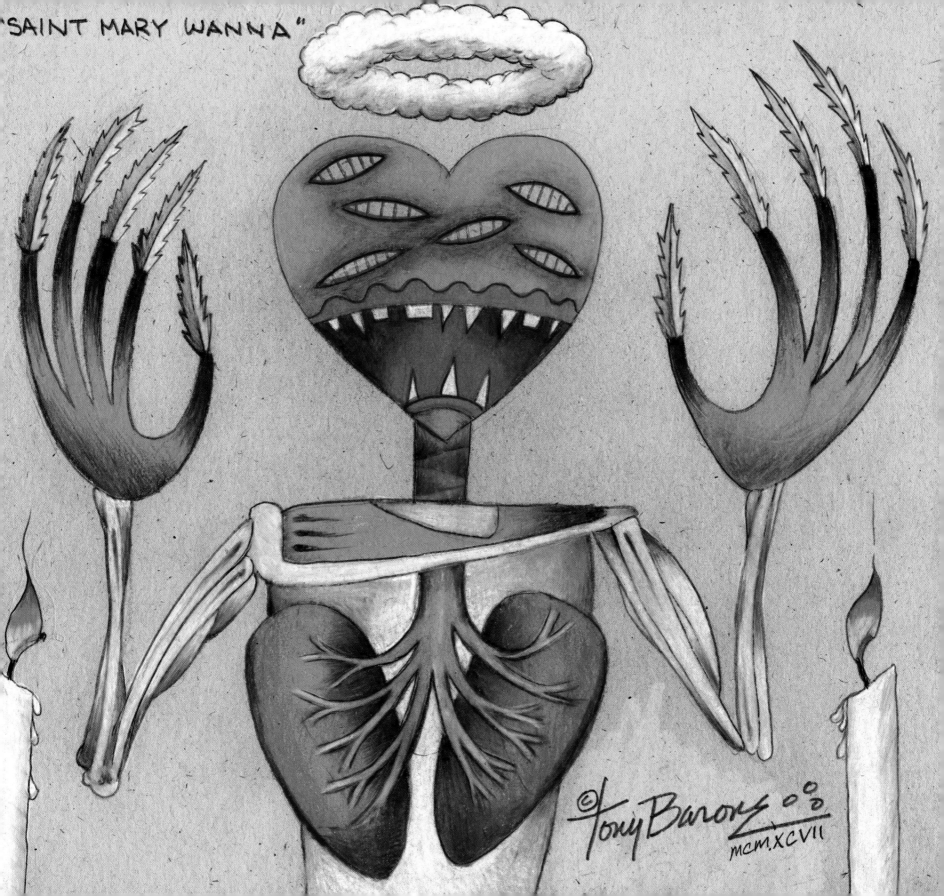

"After getting out of college, Eatie traveled to India and lived in an ashram in New Delhi where she sought divine enlightenment and the true meaning of life from her guru, the Deli Llama."

"LOVE MONSTER SEEKING THE TRUTH OF THE DELI LLAMA"
2000 #154

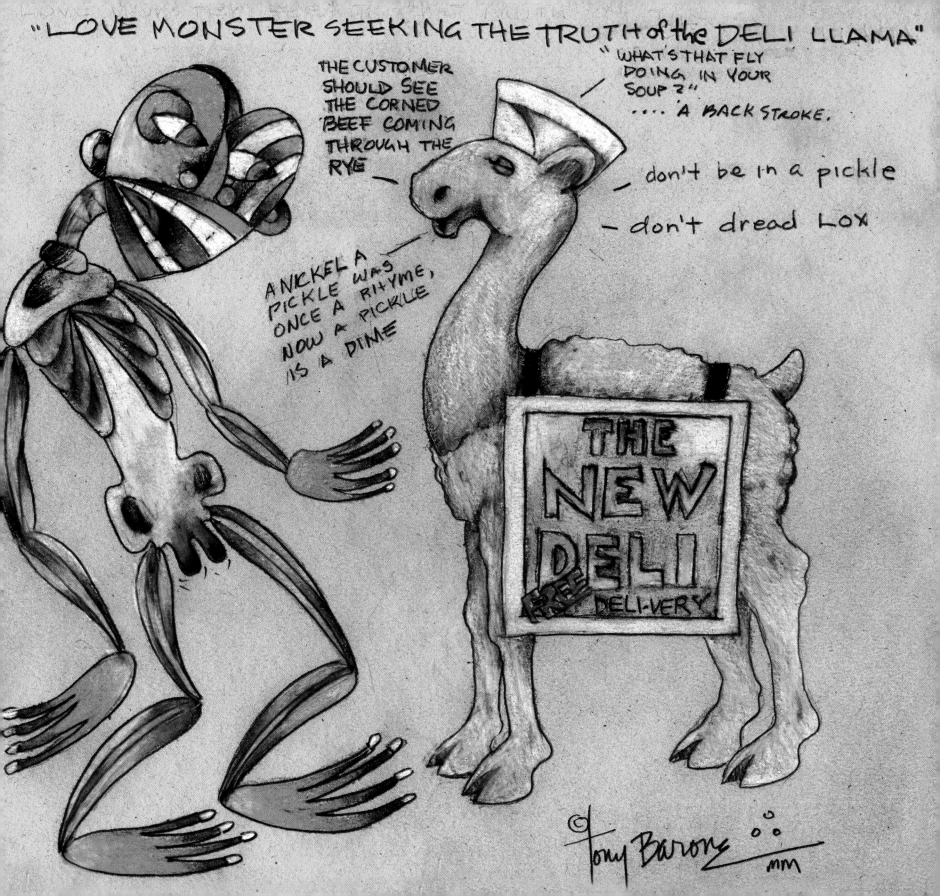

"Eatie Wright could not stand the 'ignorance and stupidity' of tobacco smokers. She was angered at their 'rudeness' when they would light up in public. In an effort to simultaneously vent her anger and offer some constructive advice, she once verbally attacked a German tourist, who lit a stogie at a cafe table near where she was lunching, by calling him a 'doom cough.'"

"DOOM COUGH"
1997 #61

©Tony Barone
MCMXCVII

"DOOM COUGH"

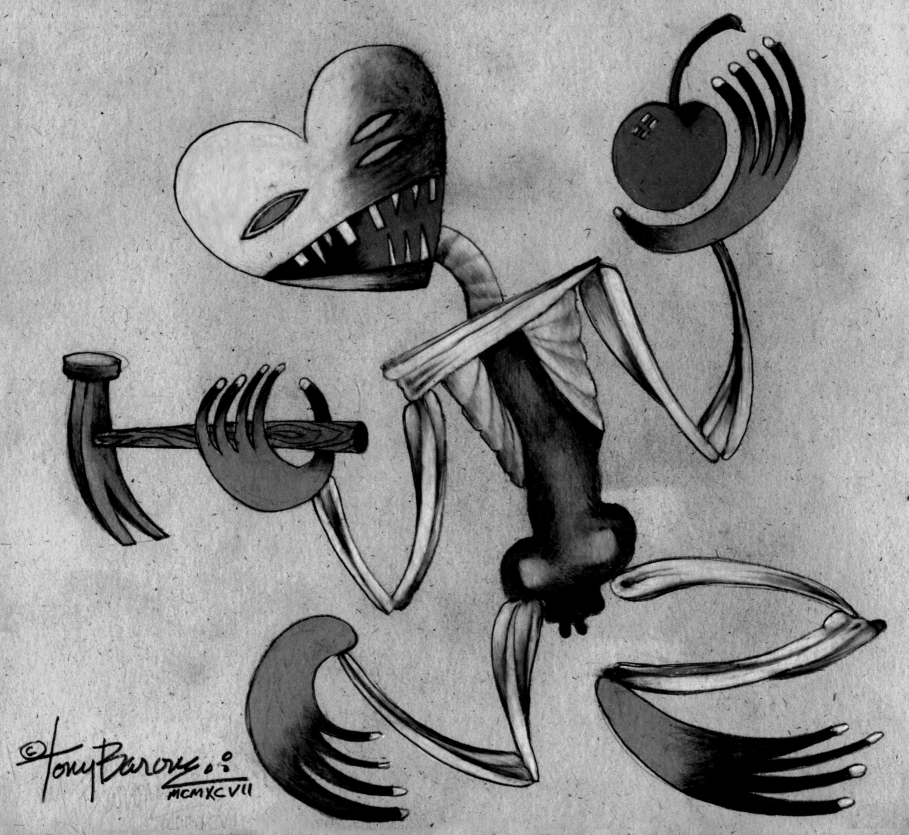

CHAPTER IV
CHERRY CORDIAL (KAHN)

THE KAHN FAMILY DAUGHTER

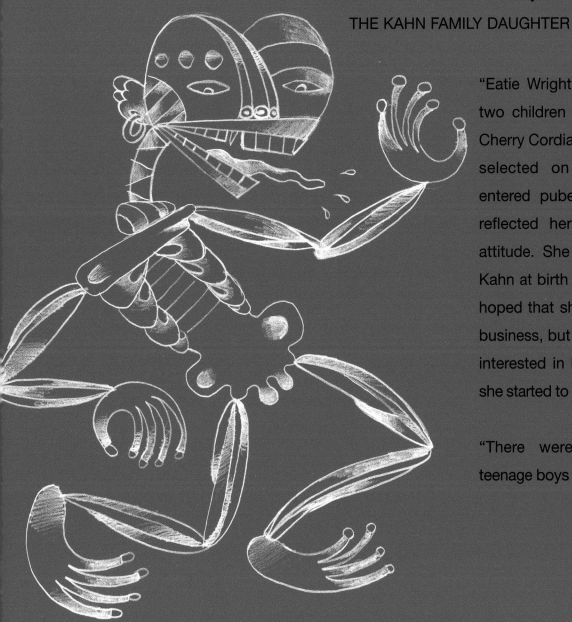

"Eatie Wright and X. Kahn's first of two children was a daughter called Cherry Cordial (Kahn), a name Cherry selected on her own when she entered puberty. To her, the name reflected her sweet and flirtatious attitude. She had been named Mia Kahn at birth because her father had hoped that she would join him in his business, but Cherry was much more interested in boys than burglary and she started to date soon after puberty."

"There were many attempts by teenage boys to bust Cherry's cherry."

"LOVE MONSTER BUSTING ITS CHERRY"
1997 #21

"In college, Cherry Cordial took a drama class that turned out to be a disaster. When she was quizzed on what she thought about Chekhov, she responded: 'Why do I need a Russian things-to-do list? I'm not planning a trip to Moscow.'"

"LOVE MONSTER THINKING CHEKHOV IS A RUSSIAN THINGS-TO-DO LIST"
2002 #165

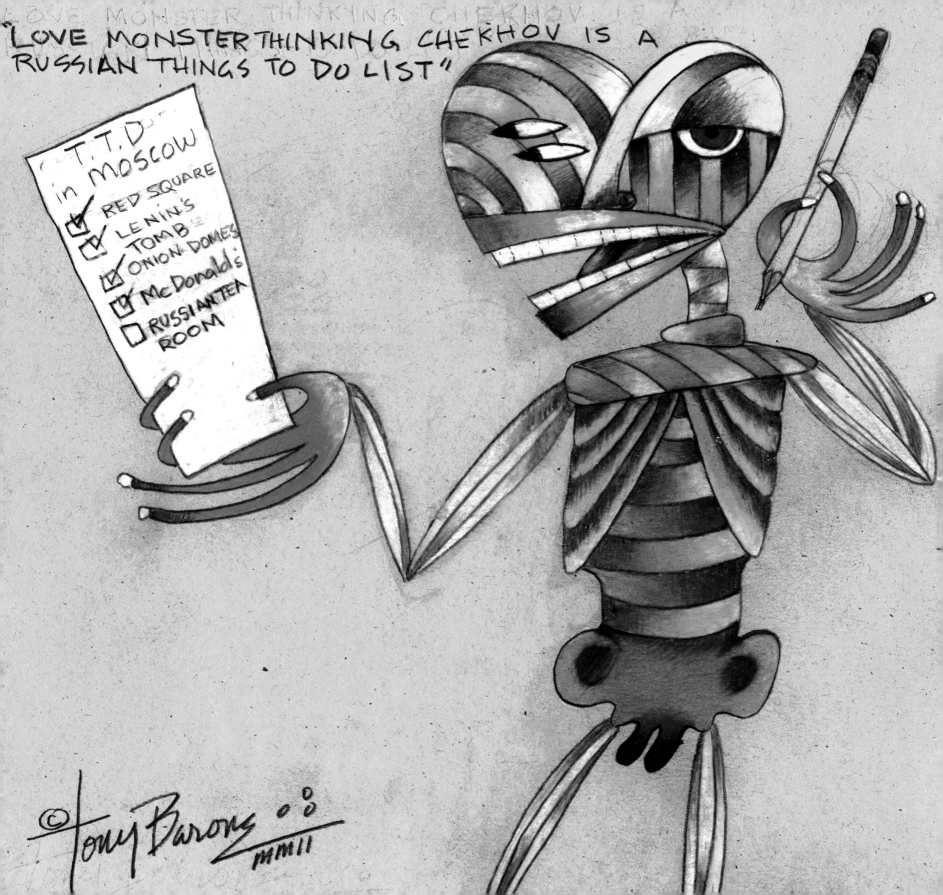

"Cherry Cordial, like most of her Hollywood friends, had made the decision to get breast implants. Wanting more jiggle and bounce to the ounce, she avoided using silicon or saline and went for Silly Putty."

"LOVE MONSTER WITH SILLY PUTTY BREAST IMPLANTS"
1997 #32

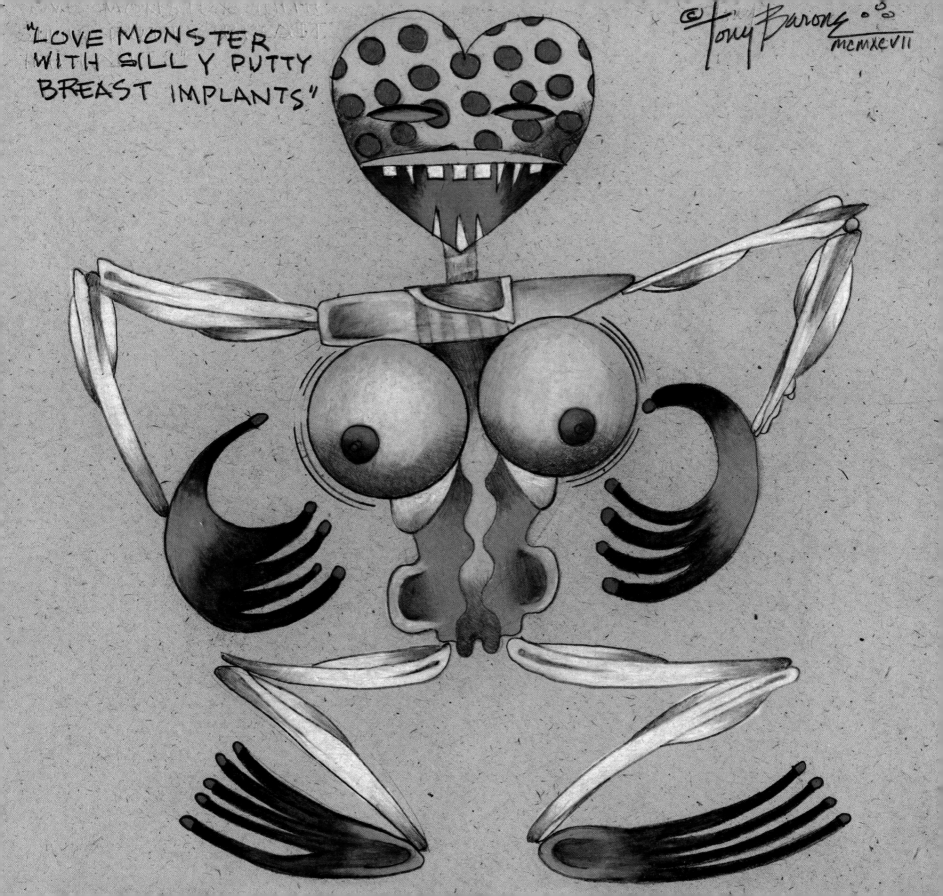

"Cherry Cordial was convinced her new store-bought breasts did the job when she attracted a slick and cocky nouveau riche Silicon Valley entre-manure with a breast fixation. She dated him until his I.P.O. turned to shit."

"LOVE MONSTER AS A SILICON VALLEY ENTRE MANURE WHOSE I.P.O. HAS JUST TURNED TO SHIT"
2000 #145

"LOVE MONSTER AS A SILICON VALLEY ENTRE MANURE WHOSE IPO HAS JUST TURNED TO SHIT"

"Cherry Cordial's younger brother was always a nuisance around the cave. He was constantly taunting her, calling her 'crabby' and 'shell-fish.'"

"LOVE MONSTER BEING SHELL-FISH AND CRABBY"
2000 #153

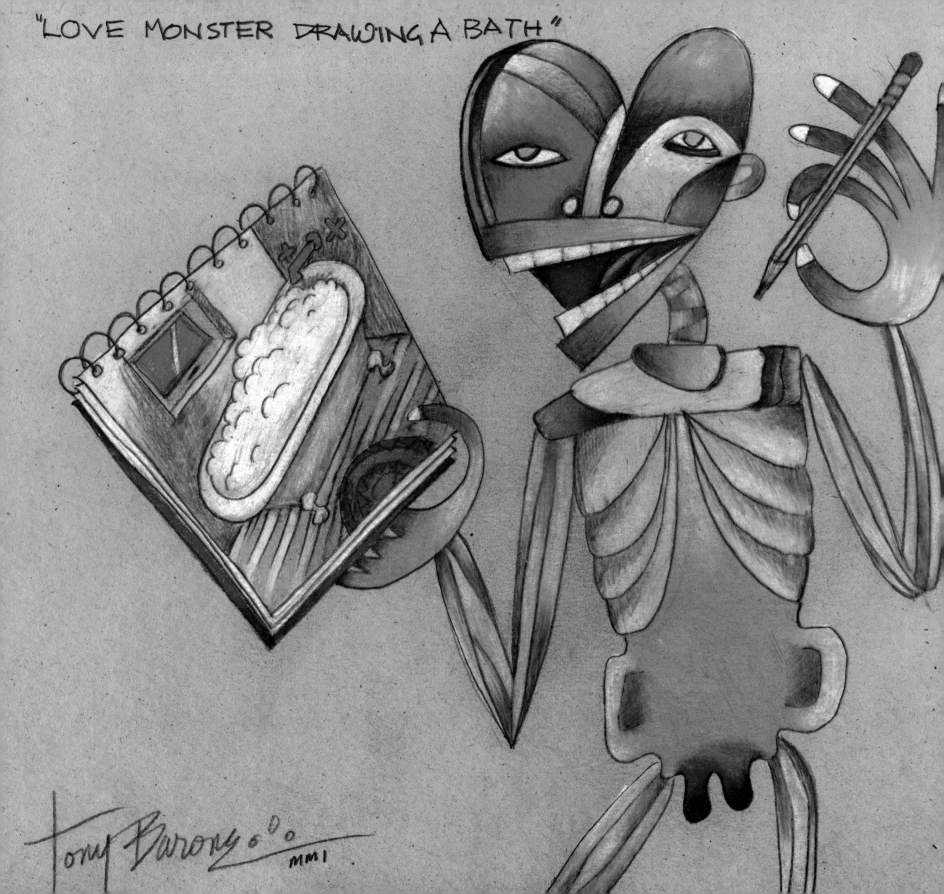

CHAPTER V
E. NUFF KAHN

THE KAHN FAMILY SON

"Eatie Wright and X. Kahn's younger of their two children was a son that they named E. Nuff Kahn. They had hoped that he would inherit his father's artistic ability, preferably without his father's underworld vices. In other words, they hoped he would be a 'legitimate artist' instead of a con artist. Apparently E. Nuff was born with his father's artistic gifts because many of the cave paintings found in the Kahn family digs, the 'Kahn-cave,' can be attributed to E. Nuff. One such cave painting shows E. Nuff exercising his painterly talents by drawing a bath."

"LOVE MONSTER DRAWING A BATH"
2001 #163

"In many ways, E. Nuff Kahn was a typical teenage boy. His room was messy and his clothes were sloppy. His mom was constantly after him to put on a clean pair of drawers."

"LOVE MONSTER WEARING A CLEAN PAIR OF DRAWERS"
1999 #133

"LOVE MONSTER WEARING A CLEAN PAIR OF DRAWERS"

"E. Nuff always thought of his family as being disk-functional, fully capable of operating CD's & computers. He was a typical computer kid who was always surfing the Internet, downloading music, and snacking on computer chips."

"LOVE MONSTER SNACKING ON COMPUTER CHIPS"
1999 #136

"In addition to eating junk food, E. Nuff had some really disgusting habits, like drinking soda out of a can."

"LOVE MONSTER DRINKING SODA OUT OF A CAN"
2002 #171

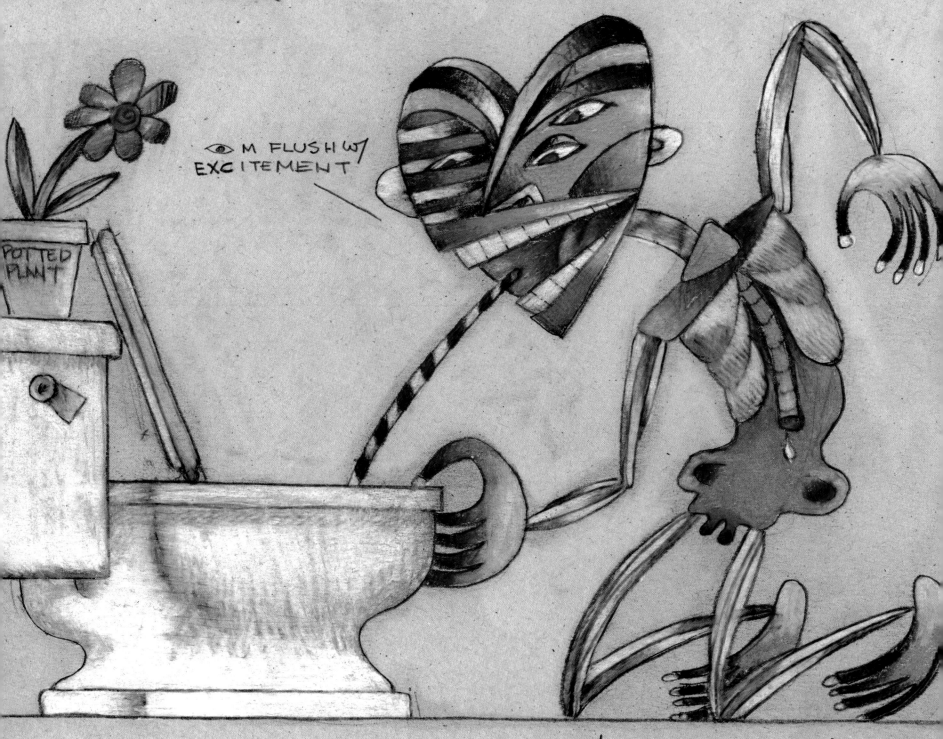

"E. Nuff got a job after school at a Hollywood supermarket. He said it was 'for the money' but, in reality, it was just so he could check out chicks."

"LOVE MONSTER CHECKING OUT CHICKS @ THE SUPERMARKET"
2002 #168

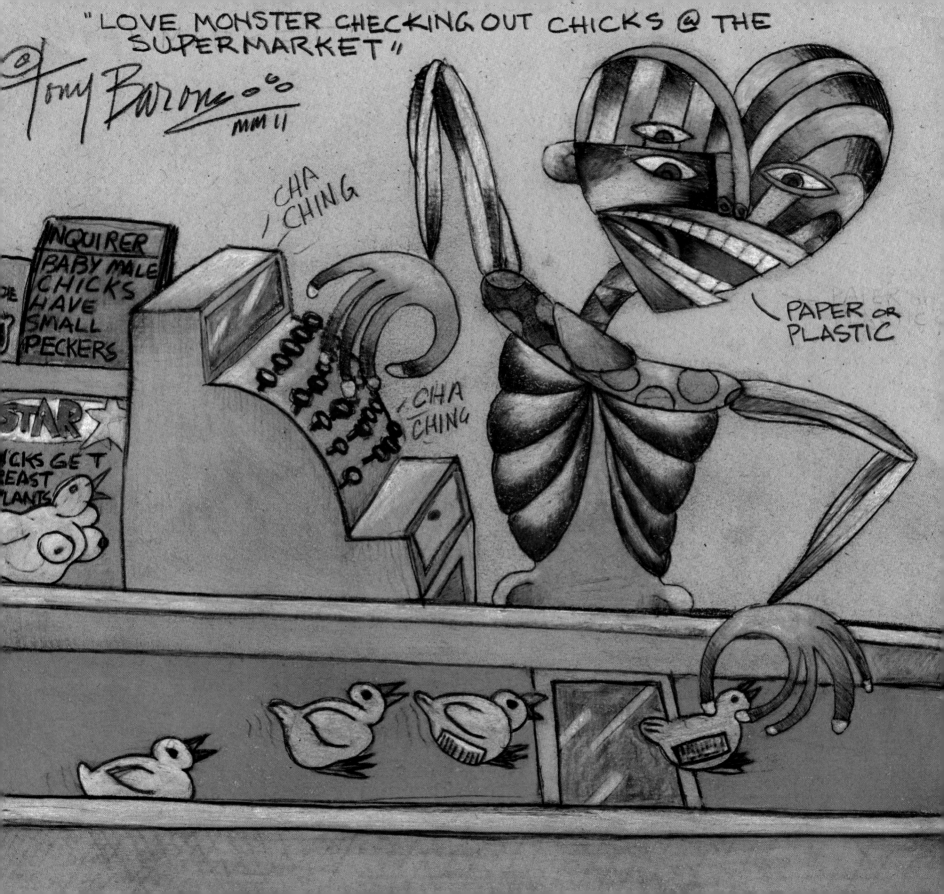

"The pubescent E. Nuff Kahn's hormones were exploding. All he could think about were chicks, chicks, chicks. When he came across a great looking chick with breast implants, he totally flipped out. He clumsily and unsuccessfully tried feeding her a line. Calling her a chick ruffled her feathers."

"LOVE MONSTER FEEDING A LINE TO A GREAT LOOKING CHICK WITH BREAST IMPLANTS"
2002 #169

"E. Nuff did not receive any sex education in school. Most of what he learned about sex came from Ima Hooker, the Kahn family's 'working girl' next door neighbor. Once, while spying on Ima from the bushes, he saw a carpenter, who had been working on her entrance, give a big fluffy beaver a screw."

**"LOVE MONSTER ON ITS KNEES GIVING
A BIG FLUFFY BEAVER A SCREW"**
1999 #129

"One day, while spying on Ima Hooker, the high priced prostitute next door, E. Nuff was distressed to see his father with his face in his neighbor's bush."

"LOVE MONSTER WITH ITS FACE IN ITS NEIGHBOR'S BUSH"
2000 #143

CHAPTER VI
THE KAHN FAMILY PETS

"The Kahn family had many pets. Eatie Wright was an animal rights activist and always bringing home strays. Her husband, X. Kahn, knowing how much she loved animals, saw it as his duty to always get Eatie a new pet on every special occasion. X. Kahn thought by doing this he was practicing animal husbandry."

"LOVE MONSTER PRACTICING ANIMAL HUSBANDRY"
2002 #179

"The family dog was a melon-collie, a rare crossbreed. It had a split personality and was a manic depressant. The melon-collie's vet recommended that it be fed 'Pro-sack,' a bulk dog food for neurotic canines that is recommended by professional veterinary psychiatrists worldwide. The sign over the melon-collie's dog house tells it all: 'Danger, bone-a-fide neurotic.'"

"LOVE MONSTER'S PET MELON-COLLIE"
1999 #107

"In addition to the melon-collie, the Kahns had two cats. The first was the Kahn family dog's arch enemy, a feline called 'Cat-scan.' Cat-scan was a totally transparent, radioactive animal, whose life was cat-astrophic. Cat-scan had used up all of its 9 lives at least 10 times."

"(LOVE MONSTER'S PET) CAT SCAN"
1999 #119

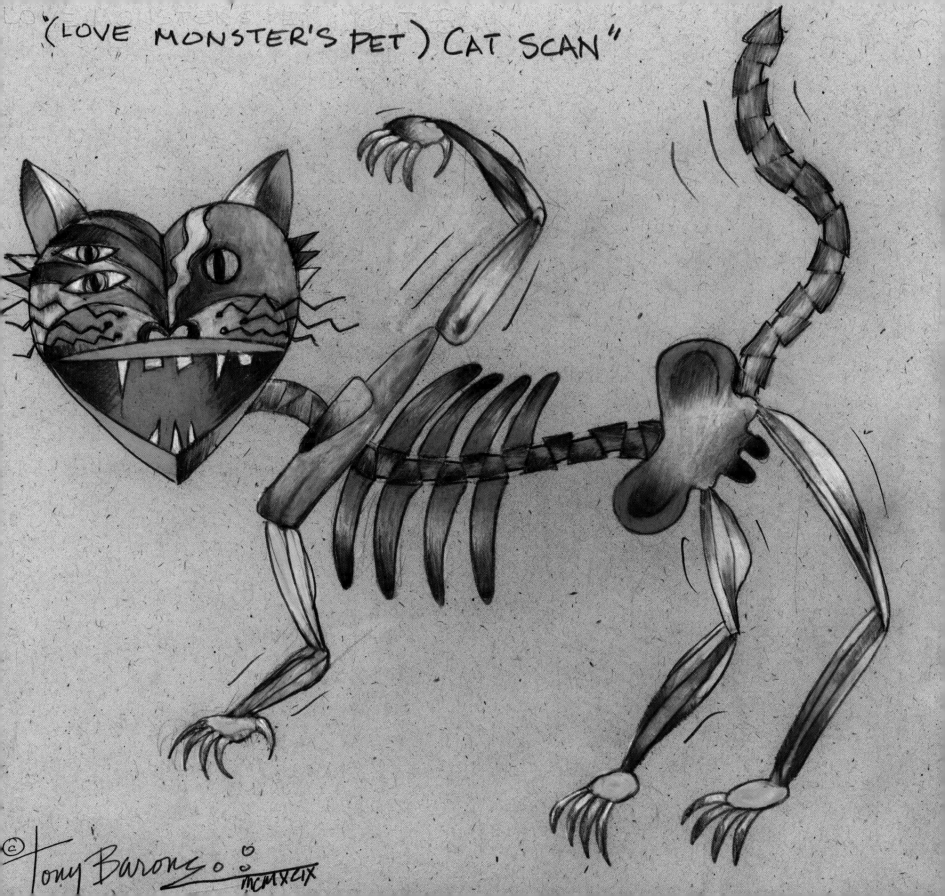

"(LOVE MONSTER'S PET) CAT SCAN"

© Tony Barone MCMXCIX

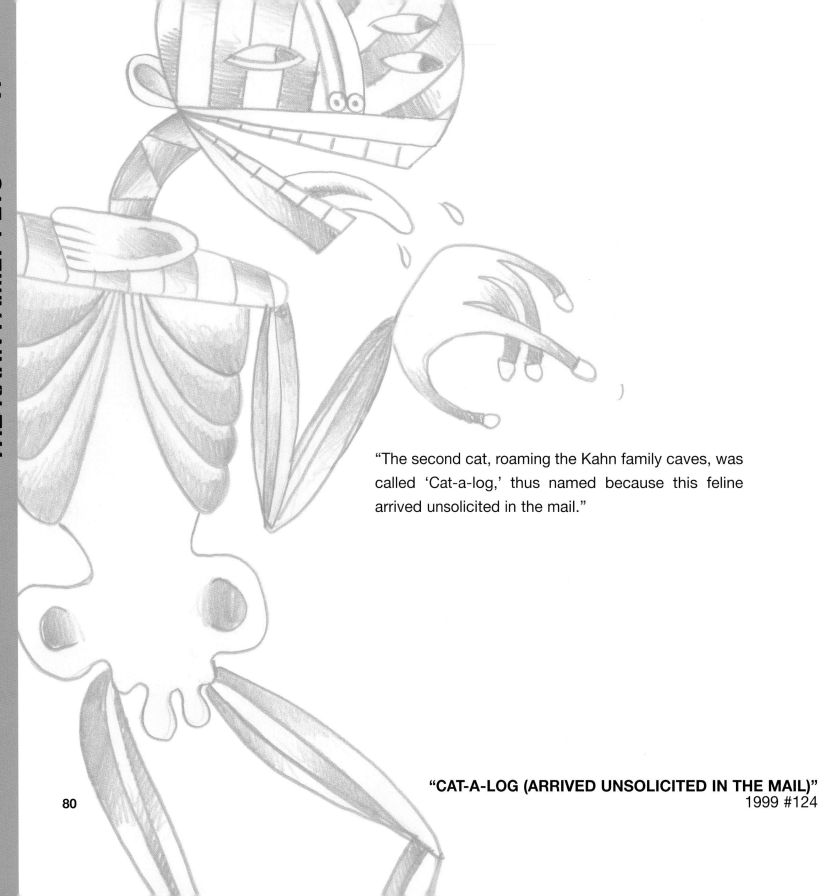

"The second cat, roaming the Kahn family caves, was called 'Cat-a-log,' thus named because this feline arrived unsolicited in the mail."

"CAT-A-LOG (ARRIVED UNSOLICITED IN THE MAIL)"
1999 #124

"CAT-A-LOG (ARRIVED UNSOLICITED IN THE MAIL)"

"The Kahns, with their fondness for stray and rejected animals, took in a rooster. The rooster had a big pecker. It had been a stand-in body double during the filming of 'Boogie Nights' but unfortunately, before the film climaxed, he had been layed-off."

"LOVE MONSTER TALKING TO A ROOSTER W/ A BIG PECKER"
2001 #158

CHAPTER VII

POLITICS MOST UNUSUAL

. . . talk about strange bedfellows?

"Love Monsters did not have a high regard for politicians. They felt that politicians were infected with foot-in-mouth disease."

"LOVE MONSTER AS A POLITICIAN W/ FOOT IN MOUTH DISEASE"
2002 #177

"Lesbian Love Monsters were very active in national politics, and like their gay counterparts, would enthusiastically get behind their favorite candidate."

"LESBIAN LOVE MONSTERS AT A POLITICAL RALLY"
2000 #140

"Because politics is 'the art of the possible,' politicians are always finding themselves bowing to pressure."

"LOVE MONSTER BOWING TO PRESSURE"
1997 #73

"Love Monsters jumped on the bandwagon to enact campaign spending reform because free spending lobbyists had enormous influence on Washington politicians. Especially influential was the Movie Theater Lobby, the Apartment Building Lobby, and, most of all, the Hotel Lobby. Love Monsters were particularly irked when lobbyists fed the presidential seal."

"LOVE MONSTER FEEDING THE PRESIDENTIAL SEAL"
1998 #80

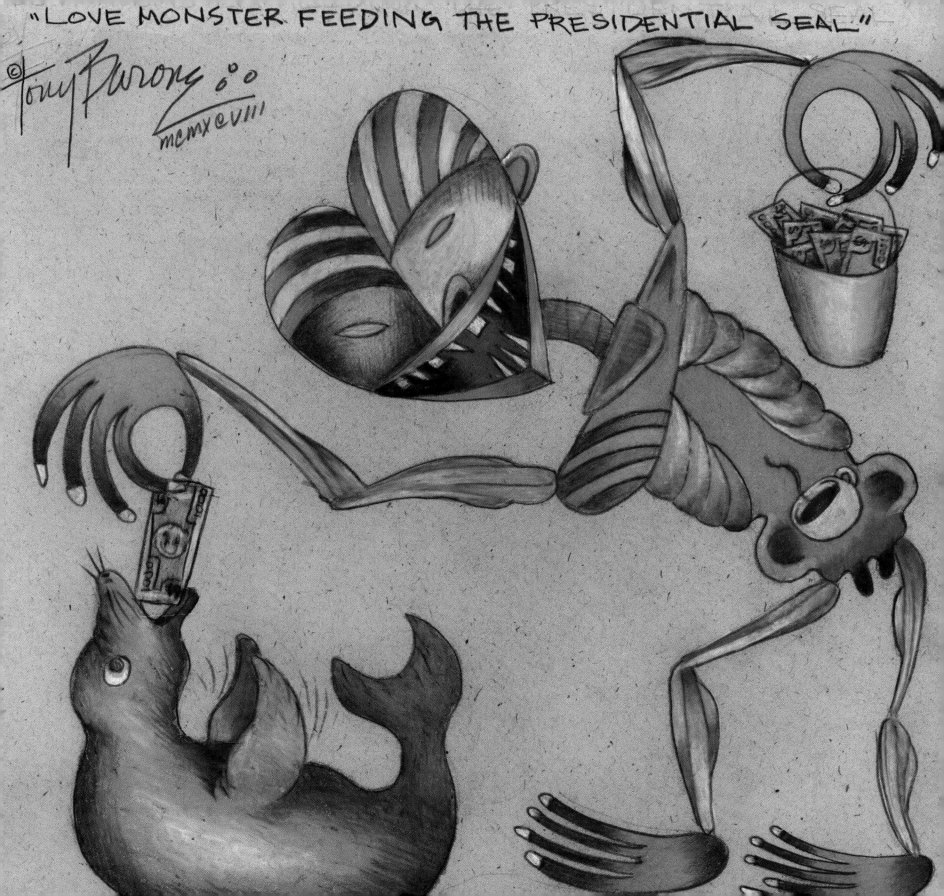

"LOVE MONSTER FEEDING THE PRESIDENTIAL SEAL"

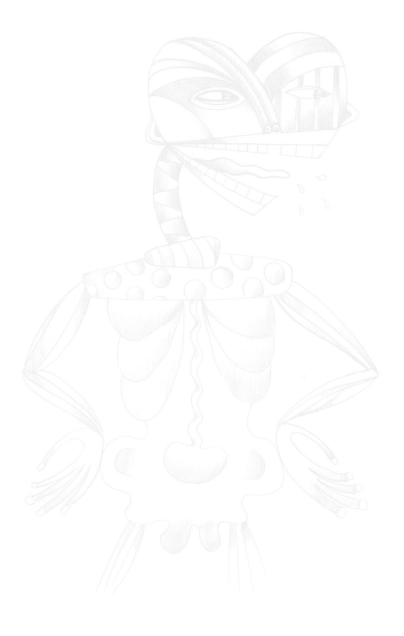

"One American president frequently received heads of state. Actually, he was adept at receiving any kind of head. I don't want to mention the president by name; but I will just say that he was in office during the Clinton Administration, and, under oath, denied receiving head from a young female intern in the White Wash, check that, I meant in the White House. In Washington, a town where exaggeration and lying has been elevated to a high art, this president was labeled a Washington   D.C.-ver."

"WASHINGTON D.C. . . . VER"
1998 #83

CHAPTER VIII
BIGGY BALLS & SANDY BALLS

THE KAHN FAMILY NEIGHBORS ONE CAVE TO THE EAST

"Biggy Balls & Sandy Balls, the Kahn family neighbors, one cave to the East, were golf fanatics. Both were swingers on the greens and in the bedroom. Biggy Balls & his wife, Sandy, were always trying to get the Kahns into a foursome."

"FOURSOME FOREPLAY"
1997 #30

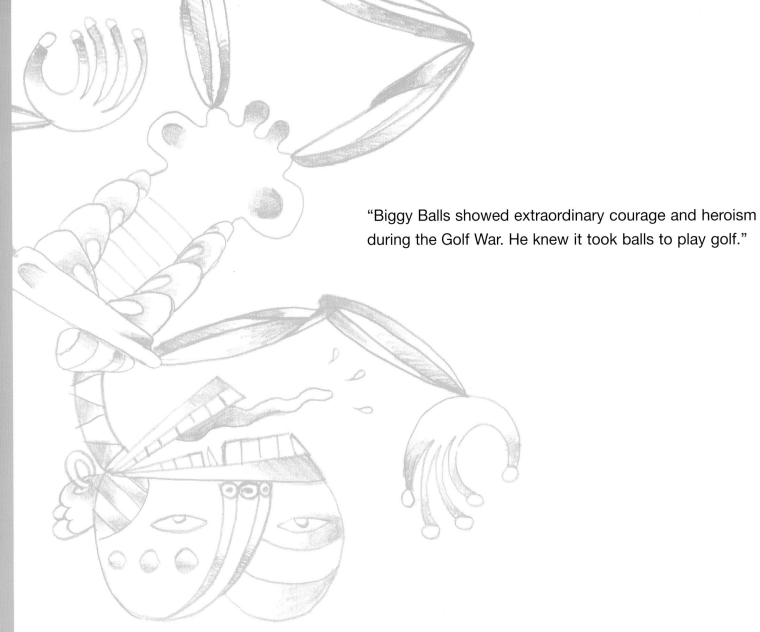

"Biggy Balls showed extraordinary courage and heroism during the Golf War. He knew it took balls to play golf."

"LOVE MONSTER AS A GOLFER W/ GOLF BALLS"
2002 #189

"Although Biggy Balls had illusions of grandeur,
he was often distracted by his short putts."

"LOVE MONSTER THINKING WITH ITS PUTZ"
2002 #191

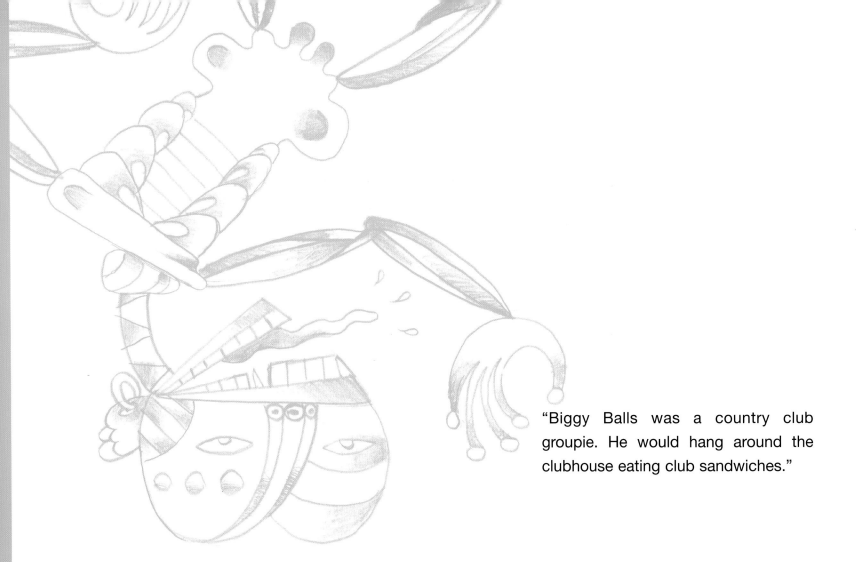

"Biggy Balls was a country club groupie. He would hang around the clubhouse eating club sandwiches."

"LOVE MONSTER AS A GOLFER EATING A CLUB SANDWICH"
2002 #190

"LOVE MONSTER AS A GOLFER EATING A CLUB SANDWICH"

"LOVE MONSTER PUMPING IRON"

CHAPTER IX
JOCK ITCHE´

EATIE WRIGHT'S PERSONAL TRAINER AND MASSAGE THERAPIST

"The Kahn family neighbor, one cave to the north, was a personal fitness trainer from France by the name of 'Jock Itche´ (pronounced Itchay). He was a championship weight lifter who worked all day and played all night. He's 'Jock around the clock.' At night Jock frequented dance clubs looking for bar belles; he loved pumping iron."

"LOVE MONSTER PUMPING IRON"
1997 #66

"Jocks like Jock can be pretty disgusting, especially in mixed company. For some unknown reason, they tend to always be playing with their basket ball.

"LOVE MONSTER PLAYING WITH ITS BASKET BALL"
1998 #92

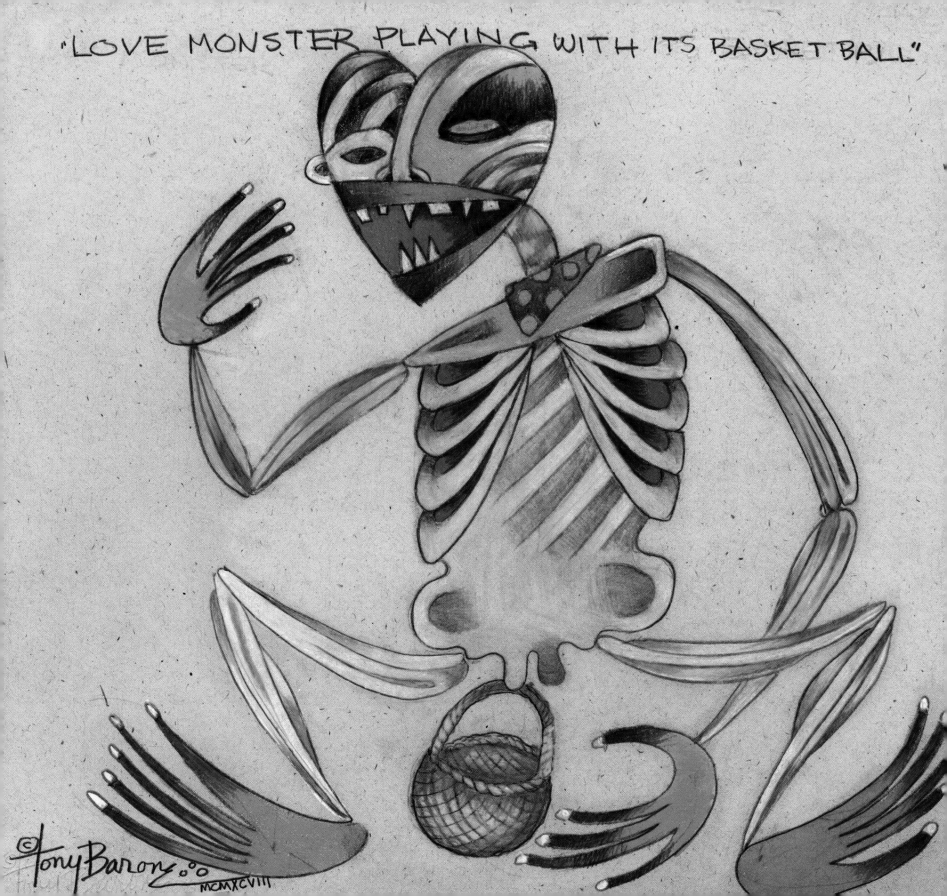

"Last January, the sports-minded Jock Itche´ hosted a Super Bowl party in his cave. Although he had prepared for days, the Super Bowl was only large enough for three guests."

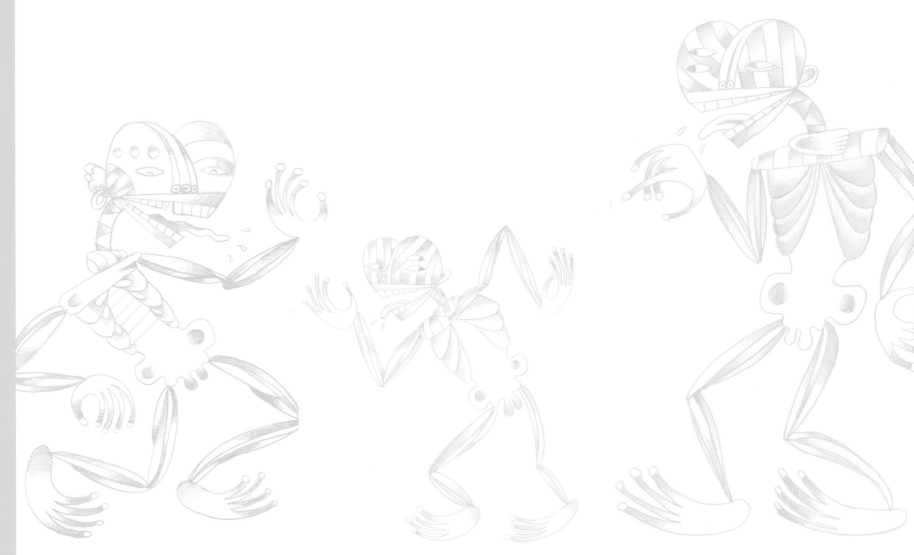

LOVE MONSTERS AT A SUPER BOWL PARTY"
1998 #98

"TRENDY LOVE MONSTER"

CHAPTER X
GORE MAY AND I. M. TRENDY

THE KAHN FAMILY'S SOCIAL CLIMBING NEIGHBORS

"The Kahn family's snooty neighbors and friends, Gore May and I. M. Trendy, were domestic partners with a pompous sybaritic lifestyle, and the best view in the Hollywood Hills (known as 'the Hills' by other 'in folks'). They were pretentious social climbers absorbed by the latest fad and every trendy 'in' thing."

"TRENDY LOVE MONSTER"
1997 #43

"Though named May Gore at birth, she reversed her given name and family name from May Gore to Gore May. Gore May had an aloof attitude and after a couple of glasses of Chardonnay would whine: 'everything European is better.' In fact, she would often get drunk and vent, thus, whining and wining simultaneously."

"LOVE MONSTER WHINING AND WINING SIMULTANEOUSLY"
1997 #55

"Gore May was a snob and a prig who was impressed with people who were rich and famous. Her 'look-down-the-nose-better-than-thou' attitude was a lot like that of a Beverly Hills shop or department store sales clerk (now called 'associate'). Although she herself did not have pedigree, wealth or fame, Gore May relished the thought of someday possessing these lofty attributes."

"LOVE MONSTER RELISHING THE THOUGHT"
1997 #77

"Gore May considered herself to be 'the hostess with the mostest.' She knew all about exotic and gourmet food: she knew where to find it, how to prepare it, and most of all, how to eat it. She would control every event, confidently tapping her glass at a cocktail party to get everyone's attention before making a toast."

"LOVE MONSTER MAKING A TOAST"
1997 #44

"Gore May preferred French cooking; the less food looked like food, the more she seemed to like it. Gore May

was enamored of exotic game; the more exotic the creature, the more excited she became about devouring it. She combined her passion for rare delicacies with advanced French cooking techniques and once got arrested for elephant poaching."

"LOVE MONSTERS CAUGHT ELEPHANT POACHING"
2000 #152

GORE MAY & I. M. TRENDY

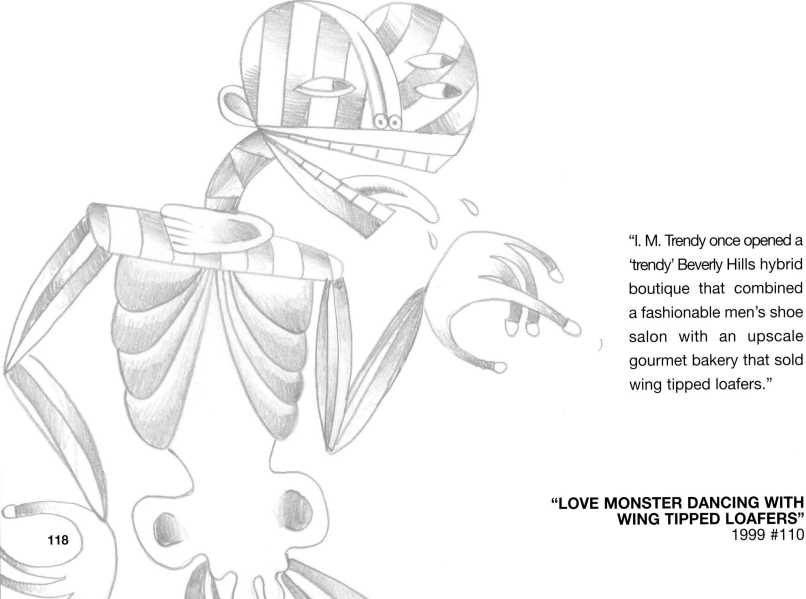

"I. M. Trendy once opened a 'trendy' Beverly Hills hybrid boutique that combined a fashionable men's shoe salon with an upscale gourmet bakery that sold wing tipped loafers."

"LOVE MONSTER DANCING WITH WING TIPPED LOAFERS"
1999 #110

"LOVE MONSTER DANCING WITH WING TIPPED LOAFERS"

Tony Barone

MCMXCIX

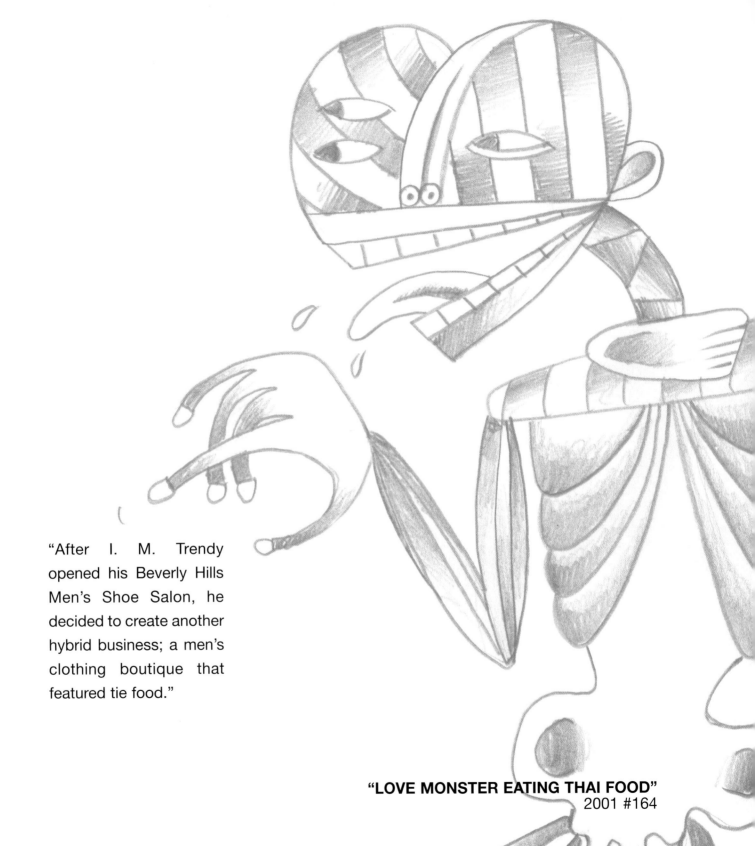

"After I. M. Trendy opened his Beverly Hills Men's Shoe Salon, he decided to create another hybrid business; a men's clothing boutique that featured tie food."

"LOVE MONSTER EATING THAI FOOD"
2001 #164

"Gore May would roam the aisles of imported food shops, a form of urban foraging. Even when she bought something that wasn't imported, she would give domestic products French names, the way many Americans called the Target stores 'Tar-je.' She would elevate Spam brand canned meat to fancy food status by referring to it as 'bull-le-tin.'"

"LOVE MONSTER READING A BULL-LE-TIN"
1999 #122

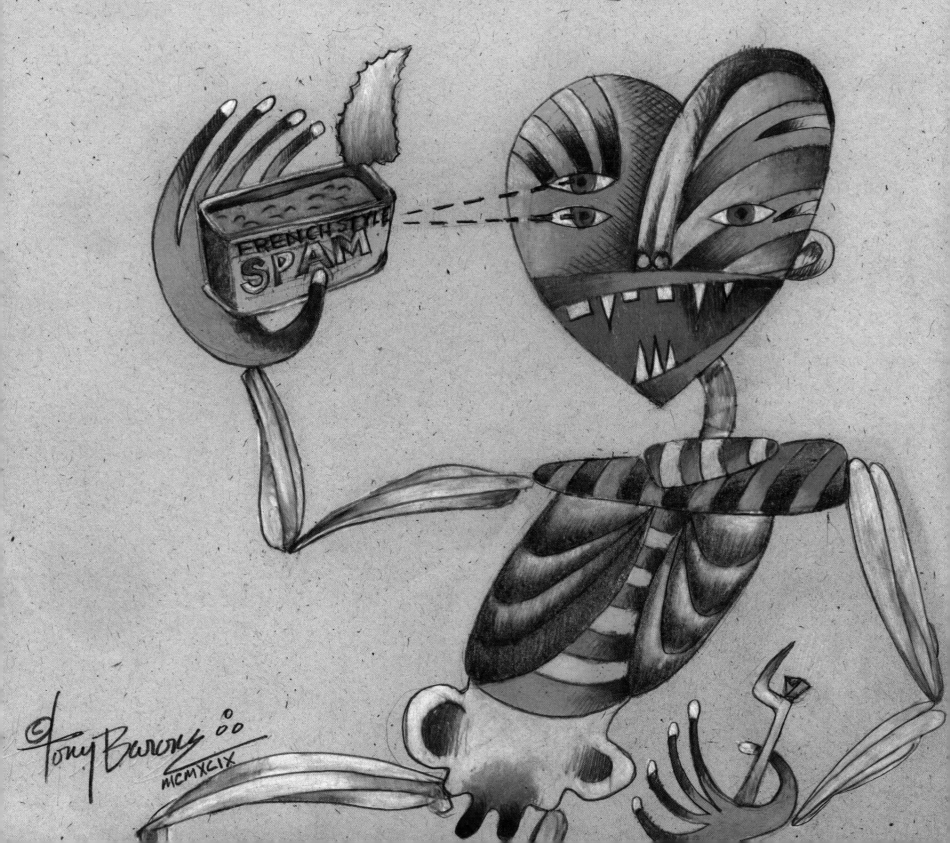

"LOVE MONSTER READING A BULL-Le-TIN"

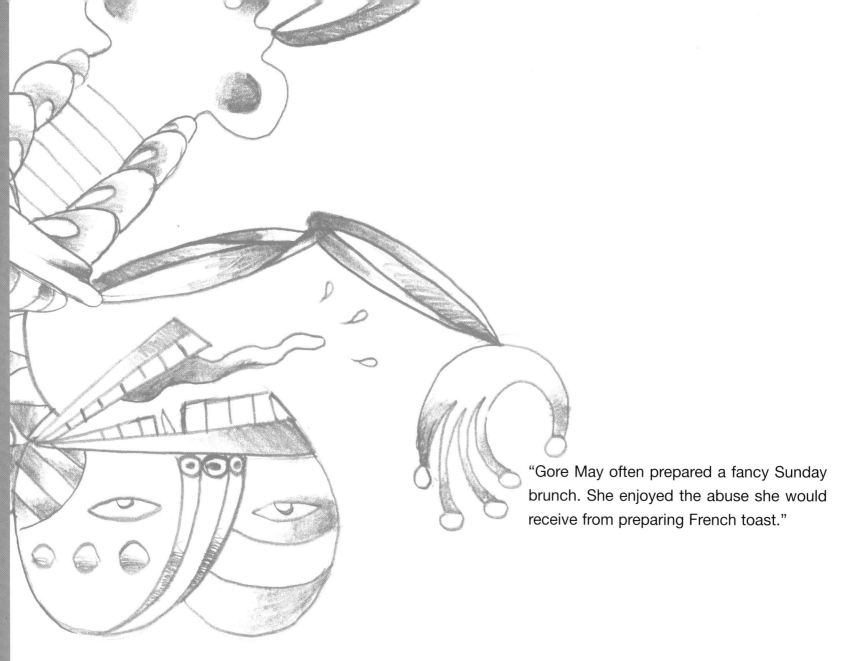

"Gore May often prepared a fancy Sunday brunch. She enjoyed the abuse she would receive from preparing French toast."

"LOVE MONSTER EATING FRENCH TOAST AND GETTING A TONGUE LASHING"
1999 #123

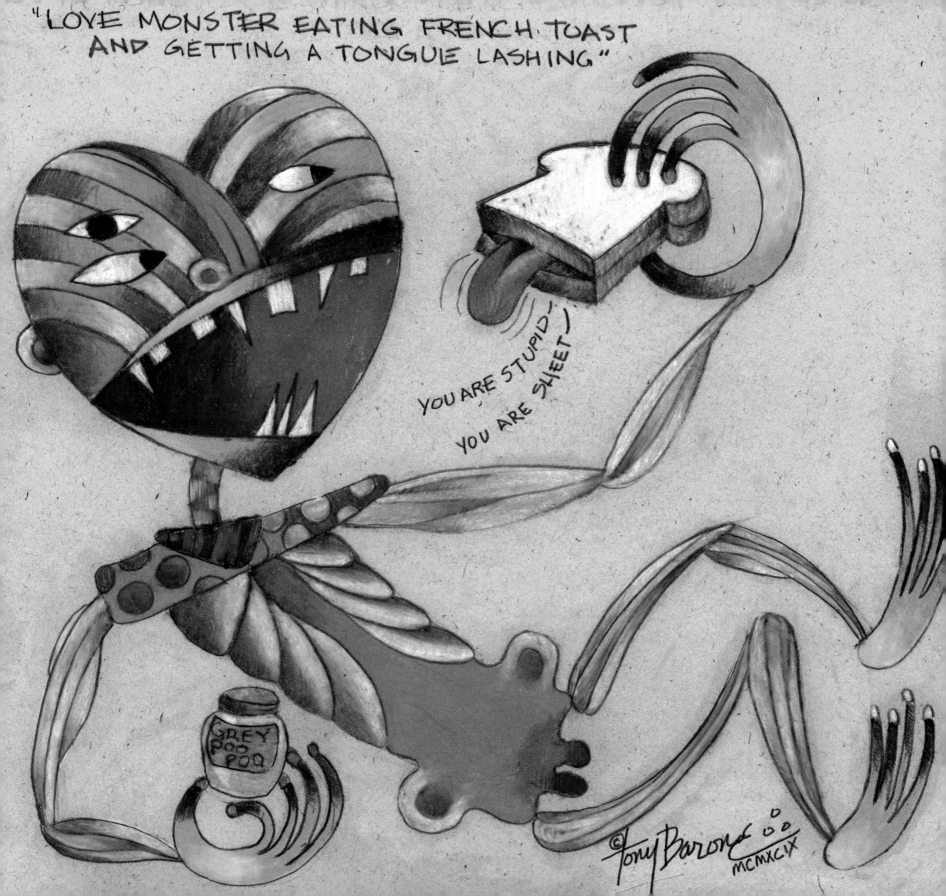

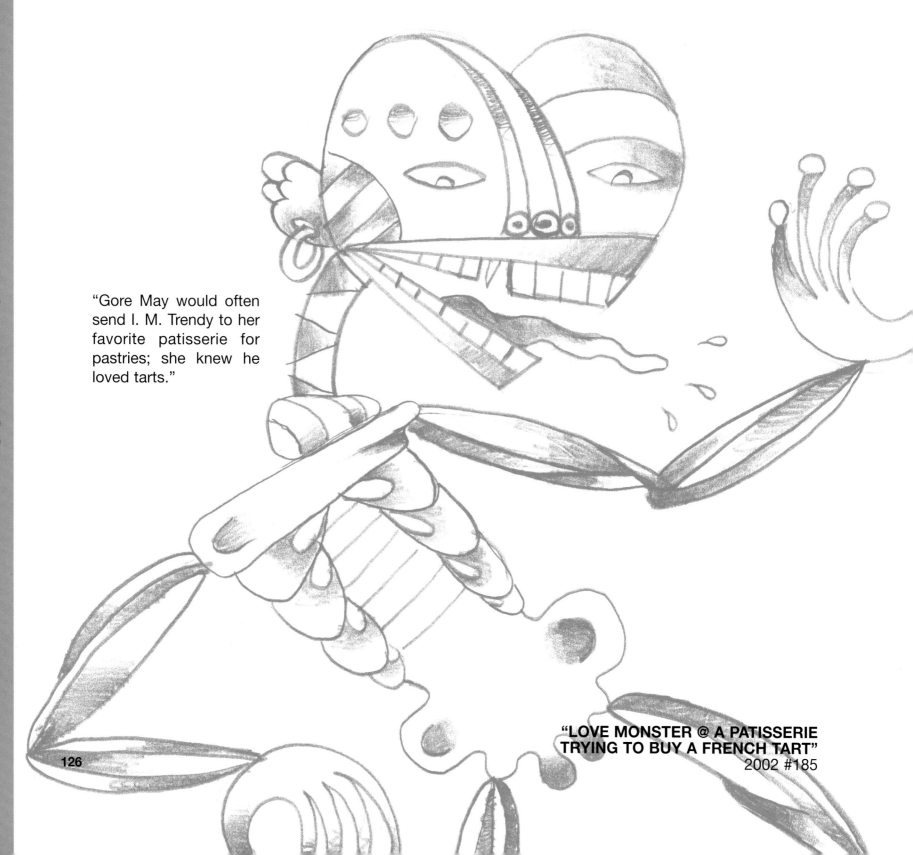

"Gore May would often send I. M. Trendy to her favorite patisserie for pastries; she knew he loved tarts."

"LOVE MONSTER @ A PATISSERIE TRYING TO BUY A FRENCH TART"
2002 #185

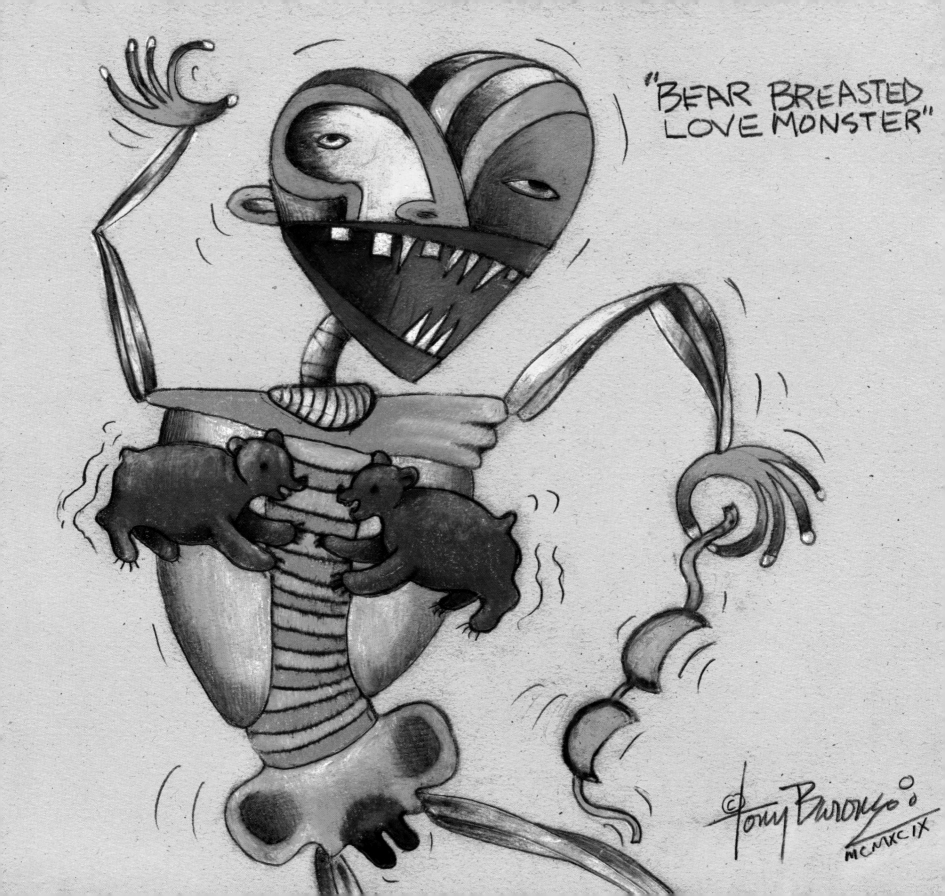

CHAPTER XI
IMA HOOKER

THE KAHN FAMILY'S GOOD HEARTED WORKING GIRL NEIGHBOR

"Ima Hooker, the Kahn's good hearted working girl neighbor two caves over, never really intended to enter the world's oldest profession. When she had gotten her pet kitty a spot promoting cat food in a national TV commercial, everything changed. After the kitty starred in the pet food ad, Ima proudly went around telling everyone she knew 'the money will soon be rollin' in' cause I'm putting my pussy to work.' When the johns heard that, they started lining up with fistfuls of cash. What's a girl to do? Ima Hooker thought about moving to a new town and starting over as a virgin. She wanted to go someplace where no one knew about her rep on the streets. After much consideration, she chose 'The Big Apple,' New York City. Being a born again virgin, she was able to land a banking job at Chaste Manhattan, however, it wasn't long before she was able to put her assets to work in the bookkeeping department at the bank. Her 'entry level position' was extremely popular with her male co-workers."

"It wasn't long before Ima Hooker pined for the streets of L.A., especially Hollywood Boulevard, where she would meet the rich and famous. She missed lounging around bare breasted at some film industry heavy hitter's palm surrounded pool in the hills."

"BEAR BREASTED LOVE MONSTER"
1999 #100

"Over the years, Ima Hooker, had discerned that most of her sailor clientele preferred girls who had 'C' cup breasts."

"LOVE MONSTER WITH BREAST IMPLANTS . . . .SEA CUP"
1997 #58

"LOVE MONSTER WITH BREAST IMPLANTS.....SEA CUP"

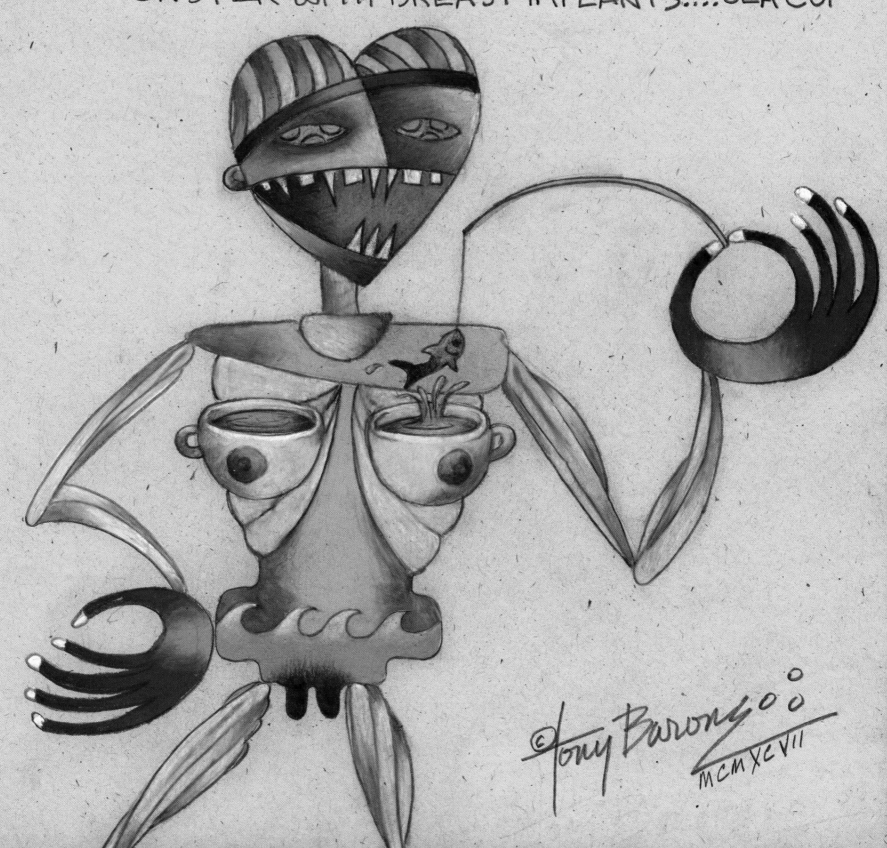

"A street walker named Edie Head was Ima Hooker's Chinese girlfriend. Before Edie Head started working Hollywood Boulevard, she tried her hand at designing costumes for Hollywood film studios. This skill came in handy when Edie needed to create fantasy attire to wear for her more discerning clients, like the johns who really like perky little tits."

"LOVE MONSTER WITH PERKY LITTLE TITS . . . .'A' CUP"
1997 #57

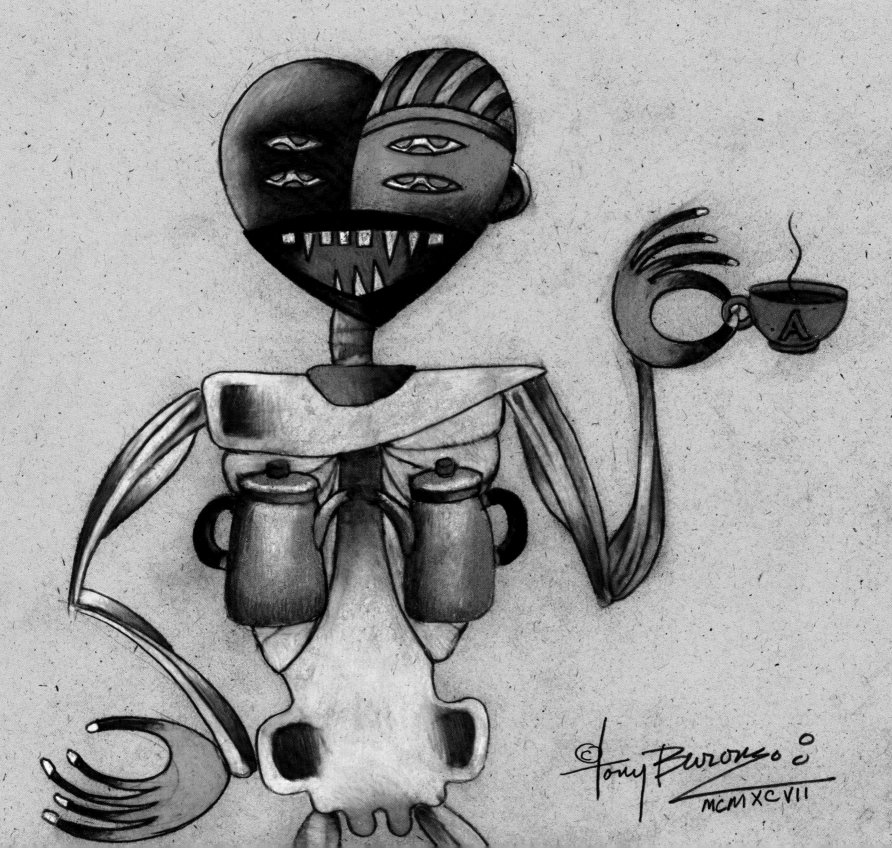

"LOVE MONSTER WITH PERKY LITTLE TITS 'A' CUP"

"LOVE MONSTER AS THE MARQUIS DE SOD....GARDENER TO THE STARS"

CHAPTER XII
MARQUIS DE SOD

GARDENER TO THE KAHN FAMILY & THE STARS

"In Hollywood, everyone has a gardener. Even though they lived in a cave, the Kahn family was no exception to this rule. They had a well manicured looking green grass carpet leading up to the entrance of the Kahn-cave. The Kahn family gardener had tons of attitude. This gardener to the stars called himself the Marquis De Sod."

**"LOVE MONSTER AS THE MARQUIS DE SOD
. . . . .GARDENER TO THE STARS"**
2002 #188

"The Marquis De Sod took the business of gardening seriously. He considered himself a well-trained professional. His resume´ included a stay in Paris where he studied whore-d'-culture."

"LOVE MONSTER AS THE MARQUIS DE SOD, IN PARIS, STUDYING WHORE D' CULTURE"
1999 #128

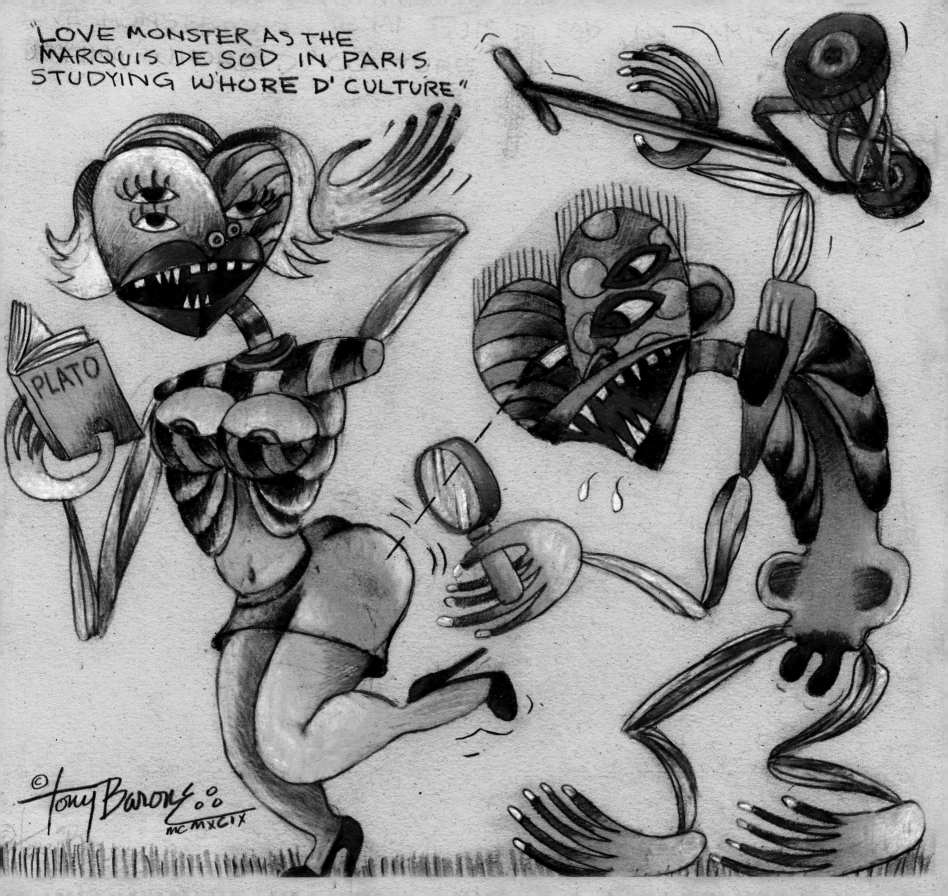

"The Marquis De Sod was a perfectionist and would only work with tools that came exclusively from yard sales. He was especially proud of himself when he would buy a garden tool dirt cheap. Once he acquired a garden hoe for 25 cents. He was so proud of his purchase that for weeks he went around town showing off his two bit hoe."

"LOVE MONSTER WITH A TWO BIT HOE"
1997 #52

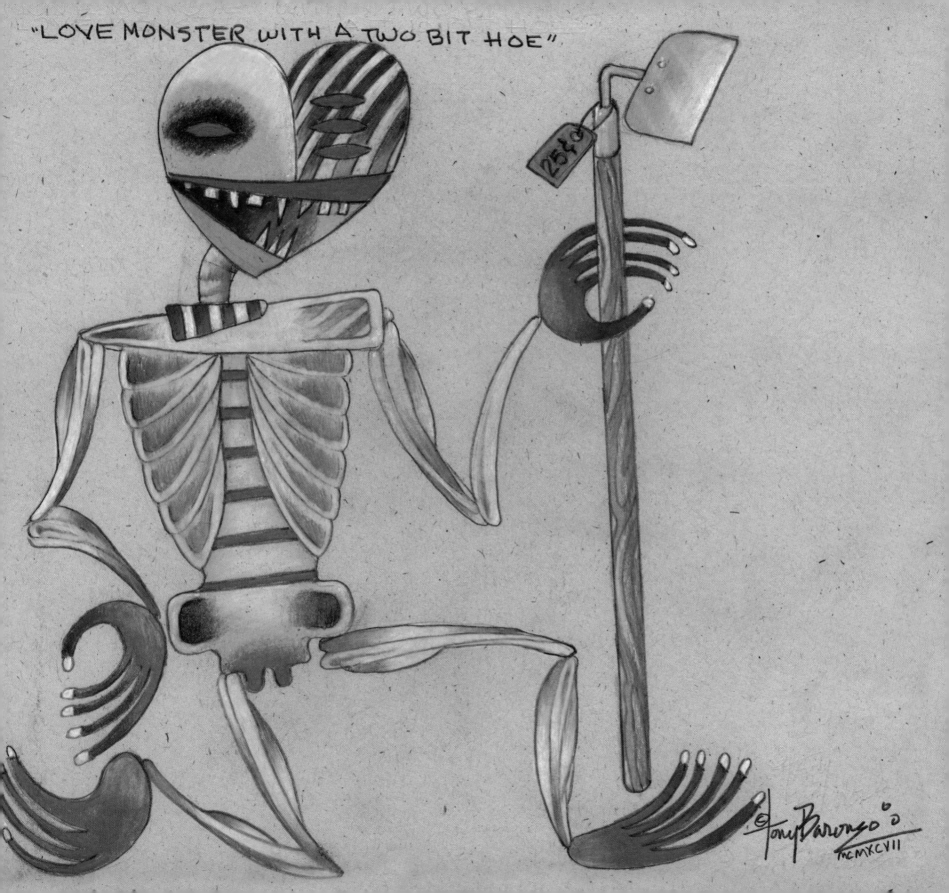

"LOVE MONSTER WITH A TWO BIT HOE"

SUMMATION

Professor Conundrum, having completed his presentation, addresses the audience in summation: "Although Shakespeare is the master of the pun, the Love Monsters, in their naivete and linguistic innocence, play at the master's game."

"LOVE MONSTER PERFORMING SHAKESPEARE"
2003 #204

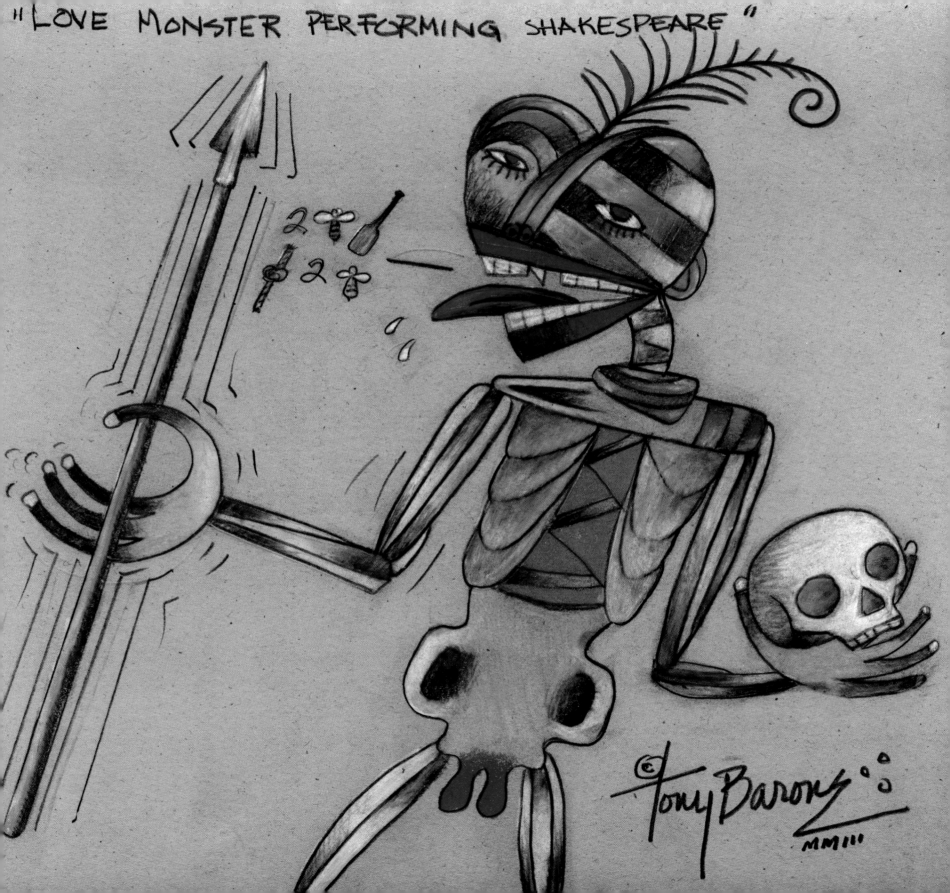